Enterprise Architecture for Digital Business

Transforming IT

Geng Lin and Lori A. MacVittie

Beijing · Boston · Farnham · Sebastopol · Tokyo

Enterprise Architecture for Digital Business

by Geng Lin and Lori A. MacVittie

Published by O'Reilly Media, Inc., 1005 Gravenstein Highway North, Sebastopol, CA 95472.

O'Reilly books may be purchased for educational, business, or sales promotional use. Online editions are also available for most titles (*http://oreilly.com*). For more information, contact our corporate/institutional sales department: 800-998-9938 or *corporate@oreilly.com*.

Acquisition Editor: Melissa Duffield	**Indexer:** Judith McConville
Development Editor: Gary O'Brien	**Interior Designer:** Monica Kamsvaag
Production Editor: Gregory Hyman	**Cover Designer:** Susan Thompson
Copyeditor: Sharon Wilkey	**Illustrator:** Kate Dullea
Proofreader: Piper Editorial Consulting, LLC	

July 2022:   First Edition

Revision History for the First Edition

2022-07-14:   First Release

See *http://oreilly.com/catalog/errata.csp?isbn=9781098121457* for release details.

978-1-098-12145-7

[LSI]

Contents

| Introduction | v |

1 | Form Follows Function | 1

2 | An Infrastructure Renaissance | 17

3 | From Marathon to Messaging | 37

4 | Operational Data Is the New Oil | 51

5 | Moving Beyond "Fight or Flight" | 65

6 | Observability and Automation | 87

7 | The Need for Speed | 107

| Afterword: Digital Changes Everything | 127

| Index | 137

Introduction

—Geng Lin, F5 CTO,
and Lori MacVittie, F5 principal technical evangelist

The destination of the digital transformation journey is a digital business.

During the first two decades of the 21st century, a digital transformation trend has driven the global economy. Over just two years—from 2019 to 2020—the pace of that transformation accelerated nearly tenfold.

The forces behind this acceleration span a broad spectrum of technological and societal changes that are not likely to slow for decades: wireless access for billions of people, the smartphone as an app platform, the increased speed and size of applications built on the cloud, the constrained number of engineers and developers, and customer demand for better, simpler experiences that empower them. The common theme of all these forces is the increased need and demand for innovation.

The outlines of this digital transformation journey are starting to take shape. What is emerging is a transformation to fully digital and automated businesses, resulting in the adaptability needed to respond to changes in the ecosystem, society, technology, and customer needs with a laser focus on customer experience, new ways of creating value, and a reshaping of the technical foundation of the businesses. At the heart of this transformation is the need to optimize business and technology for innovation.

The Innovation Equation

Today, most companies have a consistent theme of being stable at their core and innovating at the edge. If a business has a profitable product line or service, it won't gamble with the core capabilities required to support it on a whim. However, company leaders might try new ideas on a small number of customers to discover whether the new product or service has traction without risking the whole business.

This is often reflected in the amount of money spent on maintaining core capabilities, which has consumed the bulk of corporate technology budgets for decades. Even after the explosive acceleration of digital transformation due to the global pandemic, organizations still allocated significantly more budget to their core than to innovation, on average, investing only 15% of budgets on business innovation initiatives and 59% on day-to-day business operations.[1]

In a normal environment, this is not necessarily bad. But we are not in a normal environment. We have shifted into a business cycle in which organizations need to innovate.

Budget alone does not adequately express the ability of a business to adapt. A better measure is based on the capacity to engage in innovation, and that measure ultimately relies on people. The good news is that despite the additional burdens placed on IT by recent moves to a largely hybrid (remote/office) workforce, nearly half (40%) of organizations plan to expand their IT staff to meet demand.[2]

The bad news is that more people maintaining the core—keeping the lights on—does not necessarily contribute to the business's ability to innovate. For that, technology needs to be used to enable staff to focus on adding value through innovation, rather than maintaining value by sustaining the status quo.

Consider an example: a company has been in business for 40 years. It has multiple product lines that are all profitable and can launch one or two new products or services a year. Maintaining its core ties up most of the business's resources, and only a small percentage of the staff and resources are focused on developing new products or services. Most of its staff and budget are sustaining operations.

This means that the company's ability to adapt is low. The business can't take advantage of shifts in the market, putting it at a significant competitive disadvantage.

With the advent of the public cloud and subsequent adoption of its operating model, much of the core infrastructure needed to build products or run services became available as an operational cost and required minimal personnel to use.

---

1 Khalid Kark, "Maximizing the Impact of Technology Investments in the New Normal," *Deloitte Insights*, February 23, 2021, *https://oreil.ly/ell2k*.

2 Spiceworks Ziff Davis, "The 2022 State of IT," *https://oreil.ly/D795y*.

This shift was largely due to the ability of the public cloud to bear the cost of managing the infrastructure needed to deliver applications. All the budget and people dedicated to provisioning, scaling, monitoring, and operating infrastructure can be freed to focus on innovation.

But even with a jump in adaptability, we still have a significant shortage of skilled people to address market demand. A recent survey found that although half (50%) of employers are increasing hires, nearly all (92%) report difficulty finding talent with the right skills. Exacerbating the challenge is their struggle to retain existing talent in a fiercely competitive market.[3]

Organizations need to find another way to realize an order-of-magnitude jump in their capacity to innovate—not just to survive, but also thrive, in a digital economy.

Accelerating Adaptability

The goal of every business should be to achieve a budget and staff that increases the capacity to innovate. This requires more staff working on innovation than those maintaining the core. This is simply not possible for most organizations because of the following four key issues:

An operating model and culture intolerant of failure, leading to resistance to change
A majority of digital leaders (62%) see the traditional, ticket-based approach to ITOps as a waste of time because IT spends too much time figuring out how to respond to a digital incident.[4]

A security strategy based on control that requires significant resources rather than one based on adaptable risk management
An average of 46% of organizations report reductions in managing risk after adopting AI for security operations, with nearly half (44%) reporting cost reductions of up to 20% across all functions.[5]

---

3 Jason Perlow et al., "The 2021 Open Source Jobs Report" The Linux Foundation, *https://oreil.ly/xg3zu.*

4 Vivian Chan, "New Tech Leader Survey Reveals Why the Time for Real-Time Operations Is Now," PagerDuty, November 10, 2021, *https://oreil.ly/ItEok.*

5 Tara Balakrishnan et al., "The State of AI in 2020," McKinsey and Company, November 17, 2020, *https://oreil.ly/gORVN.*

Reliance on human intervention to operate applications and the infrastructure that delivers them

A plurality of tech leaders (70%) believe they need a new way to address digital incidents if they are expected to innovate.[6]

A lack of visibility into every part of the enterprise ecosystem, which hampers the ability to leverage technology that can reduce the budgetary burden of maintaining the core

The lack of insights is nearly universal. About 98 percent of IT staff and leaders report missing data critical to sustaining operations.[7]

As digital transformation drives businesses toward the goal of becoming adaptive, it must solve for these four key areas to enable adaptability and unlock the ability to innovate.

People turn to technology when economies of scale are needed. The technology changes, evolving from stone to steel to silicon, but the maxim remains intact: technology improves the efficacy and speed of business, allowing it to scale innovation.

The Role of Technology in Digital Transformation

Digital transformation is not a new phenomenon brought about by the global pandemic or the adoption of the internet, but the rate of transformation is accelerating because of the rapid advance of technology and the impact of macroeconomic and societal changes that the pandemic introduced. Today we see every industry engaged in digital transformation. From banking to retail, from media and entertainment to education, to manufacturing—virtually every industry is on a trajectory to become a digital business.

This process does not—and cannot—occur overnight. It is a journey that mirrors transformations in nature and that of a human life. A monarch butterfly, with an average lifespan of two to six weeks, can spend up to half that time in its transformational form as a chrysalis. Human beings spend one-fifth of their life growing from infancy to adulthood, with several significant transformations taking place within that period. Transformation takes time, and businesses should expect a similar experience. Human lives are often described as progressing through six distinct phases: fetus, baby, child, adolescent, adult, and

---

6 Chan, "New Tech Leader Survey Reveals Why the Time for Real-Time Operations is Now."

7 "The State of Application Strategy in 2022," F5, April 12, 2022, *https://oreil.ly/FRIOx*.

elder. Business transformation is also delineated by phases of development, each marked by distinct characteristics and activities:

Phase 1: Task automation
In this stage, digitization leads businesses to turn human-oriented business tasks to various forms of automation, which means more applications are introduced or created as part of the business flow. This began with automating well-defined, individual tasks to improve efficiencies. A common example is interactive voice response (IVR) systems that answer common questions about a product or service but may need to hand them off to a human representative. In this phase, individual tasks are automated but not consistently integrated.

Phase 2: Digital expansion
As businesses start taking advantage of cloud-native infrastructures and driving automation through their own software development, a new generation of applications supports the scaling and further expansion of their digital model. The drivers behind this phase are business leaders who become involved in application decisions designed to differentiate or provide unique customer engagement. For example, healthcare providers are increasingly integrating patient records and billing with admission, discharge, and scheduling systems. Automated appointment reminders can then eliminate manual processes. Focusing on end-to-end business process improvement is the common theme in this phase.

Phase 3: AI-assisted business
As businesses further advance on their digital journey and leverage more advanced capabilities in application platforms, business telemetry and data analytics, and machine learning (ML) and AI technologies, businesses will become AI assisted. This phase opens new areas of business productivity gains that were previously unavailable. For example, a retailer found that 10% to 20% of its failed login attempts were legitimate users struggling with the validation process. The combination of consumer tendency to abandon a brand after a single bad experience with research that finds "on average, loyal customers are worth up to 10x as much as their first purchase" means that denying access by default represents a potentially

significant revenue loss.[8] Behavioral analysis can be used to distinguish legitimate users from bots attempting to gain access. Technology and analytics have enabled AI-assisted identification of those users to let them in, boosting revenue and improving customer retention.

The inevitableness of digitization means every business will make this journey. As with human journeys, each business will experience this transformation at a different pace. At times, external forces will accelerate or decelerate this journey, as we saw during the global pandemic.

Our research, confirmed by the industry at large, indicates that most organizations today are in the second phase of their journey.[9] This phase is marked by a focus on application and operational modernization, with an increasing tendency to adopt cloud and edge technologies. This is the phase in which many will find their progress decelerated and, for some, blocked by seemingly insurmountable obstacles.

What stands in the way of completing this journey is an existing, rigid framework that governs how applications are developed, delivered, secured, and even integrated. It defines how data should be stored, accessed, and governed. It constrains infrastructure to aging standards. It makes assumptions about applications and their interactions, and about the nature of their users. Existing information architecture frameworks have existed since before the broad adoption of the internet, and well before the era of digitization we find ourselves in today.

For CIOs and IT leaders to successfully navigate the second phase of digital transformation, they must first identify key technologies and capabilities critical to enabling businesses to progress into the third and final phase of digital transformation. These capabilities include the following:

- Using infrastructure as efficiently as possible by delivering applications in a distributed model that includes private and public clouds, data centers, and edge computing
- Expanding and scaling digital operations by adopting site reliability engineering (SRE) operational practices to align technology with business outcomes

8 Douglas Karr, "Customer Retention: Statistics, Strategies, and Calculations," Martech Zone, May 19, 2021, https://oreil.ly/CvvXA.

9 F5, "The State of Application Strategy in 2022."

- Taking advantage of AI and analytics in both IT and lines of business by reimagining data architectures and governance to adapt to the convergence of operational technology (OT) and IT

- Operating securely at scale by incorporating security as a key component in every aspect of a digital business and embracing app delivery as a core disciplinary domain

Then, with a critical eye, technology leaders must reevaluate their enterprise architecture and determine how best to insert and leverage these technologies and capabilities. It is for this purpose—providing a framework for the transformation of the enterprise architecture—that we have taken on the task of writing this book.

Purpose and Scope

The purpose of this book is to explore the architecture required to successfully navigate the second phase of digital transformation. That transformation evolves the enterprise architecture into one more suited to support an increasingly data-driven and data-dependent digital business.

We've written this book for the CIO and the architect, for the IT director and the network engineer. We offer an architecture framework for transitioning IT to operate as a digital business.

We do not dive into the details or offer prescriptive advice on how—or what—to implement. Our goal is to provide a clear picture of the architectural transformation needed to enable a digital business to thrive. That transformation is determined not by us, or by any other expert, but by the technological shifts occurring in every industry and at every layer of the IT stack, which we also discuss.

In Chapter 1, we discuss the changes to existing enterprise architecture needed to infuse the capabilities required by a digital business. Each following chapter explores the trends and technologies driving changes in a specific domain. In Chapter 2, we explore the capabilities enabled by the adoption of cloud and edge technologies and the ability to adapt the deployment location of applications. We then look at the need for application delivery as an IT discipline in Chapter 3, driven by the requirement for digital business to operate safely at scale. The expansion of the data domain to embrace operational data (telemetry) and practices required to scale analytics in order to enable a digital business is the focus of Chapter 4. The rapid evolution of security is the focus of Chapter 5, in which we lay out the foundations for a modern security governance and architecture framework that infuses a security-first approach to digital business.

Chapter 6 covers the emerging need for observability and the expansion of automation from a productivity tool to an innovation accelerator. Finally, in Chapter 7, we dive into SRE as a catalyst for scaling operations in a modern, digital business.

Why We Wrote This Book

Why, indeed. As a group of leaders in a company most often identified simply with load balancing, it may surprise you to learn that F5 has been in the business of helping enterprises design, implement, optimize, and secure enterprise architecture for 25 years.

From its earliest role as a load balancer to securing, delivering, and distributing applications today, F5 has always been an integral partner with business and IT on the topic of architecture. From securing infrastructure against volumetric attacks, to defending against application attacks, to protecting a business against fraud and abuse, F5 is intimately familiar with the inner workings of enterprise architectures in every industry across the globe. In its lengthy history, F5 has also had the privilege of partnering closely with many application providers. These partnerships have been more than strategic, sales-oriented engagements. F5 has spent considerable effort to understand at a deep, technical level how these applications are deployed, delivered, and integrated with other applications and with the business itself.

Even more relevant than its technology portfolio are the leaders, technologists, architects, and strategists who have come together at F5. Hailing from wide-ranging industries—financial services, social networks, transportation, insurance, and other technology firms—the authors have expertise in every layer of the IT and digital business stack. Together, with our deep understanding of technology, we believe that we are uniquely positioned to analyze today's trends and deliver the insight necessary to identify and articulate the sweeping changes they will have on enterprise architecture.

Conventions Used in This Book

The following typographical conventions are used in this book:

Italic
    Indicates new terms, URLs, email addresses, filenames, and file extensions.

`Constant width`
    Used for program listings, as well as within paragraphs to refer to program elements such as variable or function names, databases, data types, environment variables, statements, and keywords.

O'Reilly Online Learning

 For more than 40 years, *O'Reilly Media* has provided technology and business training, knowledge, and insight to help companies succeed.

Our unique network of experts and innovators share their knowledge and expertise through books, articles, and our online learning platform. O'Reilly's online learning platform gives you on-demand access to live training courses, in-depth learning paths, interactive coding environments, and a vast collection of text and video from O'Reilly and 200+ other publishers. For more information, visit *https://oreilly.com*.

How to Contact Us

Please address comments and questions concerning this book to the publisher:

    O'Reilly Media, Inc.
    1005 Gravenstein Highway North
    Sebastopol, CA 95472
    800-998-9938 (in the United States or Canada)
    707-829-0515 (international or local)
    707-829-0104 (fax)

We have a web page for this book, where we list errata, examples, and any additional information. You can access this page at *https://oreil.ly/enterprise-architecture-for-digital-business*.

Email *bookquestions@oreilly.com* to comment or ask technical questions about this book.

For news and information about our books and courses, visit *https://oreilly.com*.

Find us on LinkedIn: *https://linkedin.com/company/oreilly-media*

Follow us on Twitter: *https://twitter.com/oreillymedia*

Watch us on YouTube: *https://www.youtube.com/oreillymedia*

Form Follows Function

—Lori MacVittie, F5 principal technical evangelist

The way businesses operate has changed over the past 20 years, with even more dramatic changes occurring in just the past 5 years. As businesses continue their rapid transformation from physical to digital, enterprise architecture must also transform to support it. As a technology leader, you will be directly or indirectly involved with guiding and executing this transformation.

This is no small task. Enterprise architecture as a discipline was established and standardized in the late 20th century, before the wide adoption of the internet and digital business models. The organization you work for likely has an enterprise architecture in place—one that was developed decades ago and has remained largely unchanged.

The 20th-century architect Louis Sullivan, mentor of the still celebrated Frank Lloyd Wright, coined the maxim, "Form follows function." This principle is often applied to software engineering, in which the "function" is the business process, and the "form" is the enterprise architecture. The premise is that if the architecture prescribes how a business operates, the business will be constrained and unable to adapt to changing conditions. Therefore, as the *function* of business transforms from physical to digital, the *form* of the enterprise architecture must also transform.

In this chapter, we discuss key technology trends driving new functions into business and the changes needed in enterprise architecture to enable a successful transformation into a digital business. Grady Booch, codeveloper of the Unified Modeling Language and creator of the Booch object-oriented software development method, says this:

Architecture represents the significant decisions, where significance is measured by cost to change.[1]

That transformation must be strategic, not only tactical, and encompass the whole of the enterprise architecture. A digital business has no component, no cog in the wheel, that does not contribute to or play a significant role in the success of the architecture. As has been true throughout history, standardization serves as a powerful transformational force, forever changing the course of industries and nations. It should be no surprise that standardization has a significant role in enterprise architecture transformation.

Standardization Spurs Innovation

Three thousand years ago, Hammurabi carved in stone a set of 282 rules standardizing commercial and judicial practices that today is remembered as the *Code of Hammurabi*. It is recognized as the first set of codified laws and standards. Hammurabi could not have known the impact this invention would eventually have on history.

Since that time, standards have been used in every era to guide, enforce, and encourage humanity in all its endeavors. From ensuring fairness of trade through gold and weight standards and protecting our well-being through safety standards, to ensuring the interoperability of devices that make the internet possible, standards have a significant impact on society, technologies, and business.

Figure 1-1 highlights several notable moments in standardization. What isn't shown is the incredible innovation that occurred as a result of that standardization. The Gutenberg printing press did more than standardize the process of printing. That standardization significantly reduced reliance on manual methods of production, which spurred greater production of books—and literacy—across societies. This led to the Protestant revolution and the Age of Enlightenment, from which the foundations for modern science developed and drove the establishment of universal education. The impact of the printing press is seen in the innovation of the "digital press," which continues to rely on principles developed by Johannes Gutenberg and innovated on to facilitate modern communication. The innovation resulting from the invention of and standardization on Gutenberg's printing press was dramatic and long-lasting.

---

1 "Grady Booch," Wikiquote, last updated May 14, 2019, *https://oreil.ly/U6U2g*.

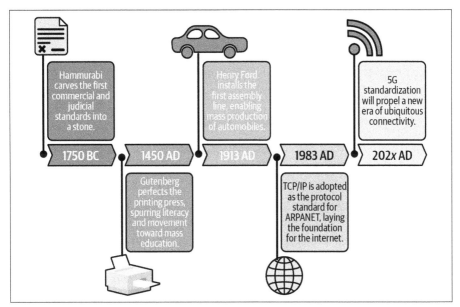

Figure 1-1. Every period of momentous innovation was preceded by a significant standardization

Standardization has served as the catalyst for the transformation of industries and societies for thousands of years. From Gutenberg to TCP/IP, from Henry Ford to the anticipated standardization of 5G, standardization has focused on efficiencies that ultimately increase the velocity of innovation.

Henry Ford's assembly line—the mechanical manifestation of standardization—is heralded as marking the start of the Industrial Revolution. While some might view his famous quote, "Any customer can have a car painted any color that he wants, so long as it is black," in a negative light, it reflects the reality that standardization of the processes automated by the assembly line required what is often viewed as compromise—but you will recognize as significant architectural decisions. Henry Ford chose efficiency and improved quality over more color options. The efficiency gained led to industry expansion that ultimately resulted in innovation as a competitive advantage. Those innovations ultimately gave us color choices and more options than Henry Ford could ever have imagined.

When businesses ran headlong into similar barriers to scale in the mid-1950s—namely, manual, tedious, human-executed processes—they turned to the modern equivalent of the assembly line: digitization. Business tasks and processes were turned into applications. For example, corporate payroll activities have long been serviced by applications. It was an early form of digitization, but digitization, nonetheless.

While this initial effort resulted in the desired growth of business, the lack of standardization into the 1980s in software, architectures, and even networking resulted in a new set of inefficiencies. Every project started from scratch, with no blueprint or guidance as to how to proceed. There were no best practices, textbooks, or reference architectures.

The Emergence of Architectural Standards

Enterprise architecture has a long history, reaching back to the 1960s when Professor Dewey Walker penned multiple manuscripts on Business Systems Planning. Perhaps inspired by the success of Henry Ford in manufacturing to standardize components and processes, one of Walker's students, John Zachman, would formulate a standardized version in the late 1980s. The principles and framework Zachman laid out would grow into the discipline we know today as enterprise architecture.

The Role of an Enterprise Architecture Framework

An *enterprise architecture framework* defines how to create and use an enterprise architecture (*https://oreil.ly/Mlf5M*). An enterprise architecture describes the business capabilities, processes, and elements needed to operate the business and then maps them to tools, technologies, and practices. An architecture framework (*https://oreil.ly/ls5qv*) provides principles and practices for creating and using the architecture description of a system. It structures architects' thinking by dividing the architecture description into domains, layers, or views, and offers models—typically, matrices and diagrams—for documenting each view. This allows for making systemic design decisions on all the components of the system and making long-term decisions around new design requirements, sustainability, and support.

While the Zachman Framework, as it is now called, is still one of the most broadly used frameworks, it is not the only one. Another effort, begun in the 1960s, would culminate in a more technical approach: *The Open Group Architecture Framework* (TOGAF). TOGAF remains the guide by which an estimated 80% of Global 50 companies design and implement the enterprise architectures on which business relies.[2] First developed in the mid-1990s and published as an official standard by the Open Group in 1995, TOGAF remains a powerful force in the industry. As recently as 2019, it has been recommended as a foundational component to cloud adoption.[3]

A Traditional Enterprise Architecture Framework

The traditional enterprise architecture framework has served organizations well into the internet age. As a technology leader, you may have been tasked with incorporating any number of emerging technologies into one of the four distinct domains that define the foundation of a traditional enterprise architecture, as shown in Figure 1-2.

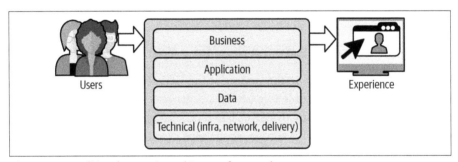

Figure 1-2. A traditional enterprise architecture framework

The four domains are as follows:

Business
Combines key business processes, governance, company structure, and strategy into a holistic view with the goal of describing a vision of business capabilities and value to be delivered. Examples include renting a car, approving a mortgage, or scheduling an appointment.

Application
Provides an overarching view of the applications needed to support the business vision. Includes describing services and interfaces.

---

2 Bob Reselman, "TOGAF and the History of Enterprise Architecture," Red Hat, September 14, 2020, *https://oreil.ly/TjRoO*.

3 Nina Anggraini et al., "Cloud Computing Adoption Strategic Planning Using ROCCA and TOGAF 9.2: A Study in Government Agency," *Procedia Computer Science* 161, no. 3 (January 2019): 1316–1324, *https://oreil.ly/13H44*.

Data

Guides the development of logical and physical data models.

Technical

Specifies the network, compute, storage, and other hardware resources required to support and enable the overall architecture.

In recent years, TOGAF has expanded from its primary technical focus to encourage a more holistic view of enterprise architecture as a way to support business strategy. This is unsurprising, as rapid and often dramatic changes in society and technology have collided and demand a new approach to enterprise architecture. While we believe the existing TOGAF is insufficient to support a digital business, it is a strong foundation on which to expand and derive a modernized version that can enable a digital business.

Key Digital Trends Indicate the Need for a New Digital Framework

It would be foolish to ignore the impact of the COVID pandemic on the digital transformation journey. While it is true that organizations have constantly adjusted business and technology strategies based on changes in society and technical advancements, no external event has accelerated change at the rate of the global reaction to the pandemic since the birth of enterprise architecture.

The resulting digital trends have dramatically impacted society, business, and technology. Digital is the new default. This is true across IT for businesses serving consumers and business alike, and acts as a forcing function to seriously evaluate the capabilities of your existing enterprise architecture. Four of these trends, detailed next, have a significant impact on the enterprise architecture.

THE DIGITAL WORKFORCE

As a result of the pandemic, 88% of all organizations worldwide mandated or encouraged remote work.[4] Nearly half (46%) of patients now use telehealth services.[5] A staggering 80% of consumers indicate that a mobile app is their primary interface for financial services.[6]

---

4 Iva Marinova, "28 Need-to-Know Remote Work Statistics of 2022," Review 42, January 17, 2022, *https://oreil.ly/eJO59*.

5 Oleg Bestsennyy et al., "Telehealth: A Quarter-Trillion-Dollar Post-COVID-19 Reality?" McKinsey and Company, July 9, 2021, *https://oreil.ly/lg2Qz*.

6 Meaghan Yuen, "State of Mobile Banking in 2022," Insider Intelligence, April 15, 2022, *https://oreil.ly/RVupA*.

Significant redistribution of the workforce has also begun, spearheaded by the technology industry. By 2025, an estimated 70% of the workforce is expected to be working remotely from home at least five days a month.[7]

While not immediately obvious, this will encourage a more geographically distributed workforce. Analysis of LinkedIn data indicates that Madison, WI, and Richmond, VA, "attracted tech talent at a rapid pace between April and October this year [2020], compared with a year prior. Madison, for instance, gained 1.77 tech workers for each one that left." Conversely, coastal cities such as Sacramento, San Francisco, and New York have seen losses of technical talent.[8] This distribution only reinforces the need for digitization, as it becomes the default engagement model across nearly every industry, including education and governments.

The impact of digitization on skills and talent is also seen inside traditional industries. Today, auto manufacturers are automating even more of the manufacturing process, leading to even greater efficiencies. But the impact on the workforce means reimagining the role of human beings, which is leading to new skill sets such as "mechatronics, a blend of mechanical and electrical engineering, computer control, and information technology."[9]

This pattern of technological change resulting in new roles and skill sets within business is repeating across every industry, with new skill sets and roles such as data scientists, SRE operations, and AI-related engineers growing as necessary technical domains within every enterprise.

STRUGGLING TO SCALE

Digital services, whether newly launched or existing, have all experienced failures to scale during the pandemic. Zoom, Microsoft 365, Microsoft Azure, Cloudflare, Slack, and gaming provider Steam all suffered significant outages in the third quarter of 2020.[10] Throughout 2021, the internet suffered several significant incidents that caused digital blackouts across the globe. Reliance on content

---

7 Caroline Castrillon, "This Is the Future of Remote Work in 2021," *Forbes*, December 27, 2020, *https://oreil.ly/GlrZ8*.

8 Riva Gold, "Where Are Tech Workers Headed?," June 2021, LinkedIn, *https://oreil.ly/aX6Mw*.

9 Steve Johnson, "6 Big Changes Are Here for Auto Manufacturers," Manufacturing.net, May 2, 2017, *https://oreil.ly/jSiwL*.

10 María F. Valenzuela Gómez, "'Unable to Connect'—The Most Significant Online Service Outages in Q3 2020," Downdetector, *https://oreil.ly/xHiCO*.

delivery network (CDN) providers for content caching and cloud application services became a topic of concern for top technology and business leaders.[11]

These disruptions are notable because of their broad and often global impact. They are more so because of the impact to productivity and collaboration in a distributed, digital workforce. Enterprises in other industries also suffer similar disruptions, but without the fanfare and headlines.

The inability to execute policies based on business outcomes puts the pressure back on people and processes, effectively reducing the benefits of automation.

SMART LIVES

Being largely confined to our homes has driven increased interest in smart devices, resulting in significant growth in usage—especially among broadband households. And if it's not interest that's driven smart home use, perhaps it's just boredom and the need to putter around the house. One-third of broadband households, and nearly half (46%) of smart door lock owners have increased usage of smart home devices during the pandemic.[12] A staggering 29 billion devices were expected to be connected to the internet by 2022.[13] That's in addition to the increase in mobile and laptop usage at home for remote work. The corporate perimeter has expanded to include our homes.

The result is an increase in data transfer. Analysts predict that by 2025, 75% of *enterprise-generated data* will be created and processed at the *edge*—outside a traditional centralized data center or cloud. That's up from just 10% in 2018.[14] The increase in data transfers as well as device penetration worldwide is expected to continue over the next five years, especially as 5G becomes more pervasive and enables ubiquitous connectivity.

---

11 Peter Judge, "Akamai Outage Was Due to 'DNS Bug,'" DatacenterDynamics, July 23, 2021, *https://oreil.ly/ZtJWe*; Nick Rockwell, "Summary of June 8 Outage," Fastly, June 8, 2021, *https://oreil.ly/9V1b7*; John Graham Cumming, "Cloudflare Outage on July 17, 2020," Cloudflare Blog, July 17, 2020, *https://oreil.ly/BKADW*.

12 Patrice Samuels et al., "Shifting Support Needs: Opportunities for Remote Solutions," Parks Associates, December 2020, *https://oreil.ly/EVuoZ*.

13 Stephanie Overby, "Edge Computing by the Numbers: 9 Compelling Stats," The Enterprisers Project, April 23, 2020, *https://oreil.ly/2OKHr*.

14 Rob van der Meulen, "What Edge Computing Means for Infrastructure and Operations Leaders," Gartner, October 3, 208, *https://oreil.ly/ZGaef*.

SHARED RISK

The mainstream adoption of digital as the default has resulted in an increase of digital identities. Nearly half (47%) of consumers opened a "new online shopping account while 35% had opened a new social media account and 31% an online bank account in 2020."[15] More than half (57%) of businesses are seeing higher losses because of account takeover fraud.[16]

But even as we focus on digital business fraud and abuse, consumers are sharing in the risk. Nearly one-fifth of consumers were affected by identity fraud last year, for a total cost to United States consumers alone of $56 billion.[17] The term "identity fraud" does not properly describe the impact to the victim. The risk to the consumer is greater than financial loss, as the impact can ripple across their entire digital identity. A negative impact to their credit score as a result of significant fraud impacts the ability to rent or buy a home, a car, and even qualify for educational assistance.

Thus, the decision to engage with a digital business is not a simple one, as consumers must willingly accept the risk to their own lives. The increased risk to business and consumers from digital transactions has grown and will continue to grow as business expands its reliance on technology.

The Impact on Architecture

Digital transformation is a *business* journey; the way businesses operate is changing. That has always been true, but the rate of that change has radically accelerated, and the impact on every domain in a traditional enterprise architecture can no longer be ignored. Consider the following impacts on the four main domains:

Business
> As a business becomes indistinguishable from the digital services that represent it, key processes, governance guidelines, organizational structure, and strategy must adapt. Digital services are rapidly becoming a product that needs as much business support as their physical counterparts.

---

15 Gilit Saporta and Shoshana Maraney, *Practical Fraud Detection* (Sebastopol, CA: O'Reilly, 2022), *https://oreil.ly/n9L3l*.

16 "2020 Fraud Trends: COVID Accelerated Digital Transactions and Fraud," Acuant, December 17, 2020, *https://oreil.ly/lypCr*.

17 Tejas Purinak, "Total Identity Fraud Losses Soar to $56 Billion in 2020," Javelin Strategy and Research, March 23, 2021, *https://oreil.ly/VfYhj*.

Application

The definition of an *application* is changing. It is now a composite of one or more logical services, the data repositories informing them, the internal and external environments in which they execute, and the security and delivery services needed to transmit their communications among all components and to the end user.

Data

Data is expanding to include operational data (telemetry). The volume and speed at which data is generated are driving the use of ML to compensate for inefficiencies in manual analysis. About 81% of business leaders agree that obtaining and analyzing more data at even greater speeds will be a future challenge,[18] and ML is one of the solutions rising to meet it. The need to react in near real time to this data is creating a need for automation to scale and secure digital services.

Technical

The computing, network, and storage resources necessary to deliver, scale, and secure applications and business services have dramatically changed the way infrastructure and application delivery are deployed, consumed, and operated. Location of data, workloads, and users is no longer centralized or fixed but includes the public cloud, edge, and endpoints. One in ten organizations already takes advantage of security and delivery technology in the data center, public cloud, and at the edge,[19] which extends to smart televisions, mobile phones, and server closets in local businesses. Chapter 2 explores the edge and its impact on infrastructure.

From the perspective of architecture, the *function* of technology is changing to meet the needs of digital business. This is akin to changes in the way we interact with digital properties and services. Three-tier web application architectures worked well when most accessed applications from a desktop-based browser. But as mobile computing became accessible and affordable, the *function* of the application changed to match the way people engaged with a mobile interface. The

---

18 Beth Stackpole, "Setting the Stage: The New World of Data," *CIO*, October 18, 2018, *https://oreil.ly/KpdZx*.

19 "The State of Application Strategy in 2021," F5, *https://oreil.ly/ZQ8AC*.

form of the application architecture adapted, embracing an API-based approach that was better able to accommodate lower bandwidth, less computing power, and smaller screen sizes.

The challenge is that traditional enterprise architecture often lacks many of the capabilities required to enable and support the integrated "digital business" model being driven by rapid societal and technological change. Like the traditional desk, the traditional enterprise architecture *function* is no longer able to meet businesses' requirements or expectations with respect to adaptability.

What is apparent, now, is that these functional changes will put pressure on organizations that cannot adequately be addressed by relying on a form designed and developed in the past. Instead, a modernized architectural framework is needed to enable technology to adapt on demand to the changing conditions, locations, capabilities, and costs of operating in a digital world.

Modernizing Architecture

Enterprise architecture touches every department, business unit, and employee. Most of today's workforce have never seen a paper paycheck or waited in line at a bank to deposit it on payday. In fact, a study on banking habits at large found that "99% of Gen Z and 98% of millennials use a mobile banking app for a wide range of tasks, including viewing account balances, checking their credit score, and depositing a check."[20] Digital attitudes are not confined to employees' lives away from work; they bring those perspectives and expectations to the digital services provided by their employer. Our economy is largely digital, which has broader impacts on business than are immediately obvious.

For example, as businesses progress on their digital transformation journeys, the digital services, and the systems that support them, will generate significant amounts of data—more than human beings can process, let alone use to make decisions. This, in turn, forces a reliance on ML and AI to rapidly analyze data and provide insights that aid in decision making. As you consider modernizing architecture, these capabilities must be taken into consideration to avoid being one of the 85% of organizations that have encountered obstacles resulting

20 Paul Lussier, "Chase 2021 Digital Banking Attitudes Study Finds Consumers Continue to Adopt Digital Banking Tools to Manage Their Finances," Chase, December 16, 2021, *https://oreil.ly/NxuY4*.

in failure despite prioritizing AI- and ML- related projects.[21] An overarching data strategy is needed, one that takes into consideration data standards, ownership, delivery, discoverability, and governance. We dive into that in Chapter 4.

All these transformations have a profound impact on the products and services available to consumers. First, many more connections exist between applications, services, and systems. These introduce challenges with security and create more data in the form of logs, metrics, and traces that must be collected, analyzed, and acted on to meet performance, availability, and security expectations. Legal implications for data arise, with respect to privacy and compliance with regulations. People must be trained to use and troubleshoot new systems quickly, as employees, partners, and customers are increasingly impatient with technology that fails. Lastly, new technologies such as containers and environments like edge computing complicate traditional processes and frustrate the ability to consistently apply policies that protect data and applications.

New skills, such as those of data scientists and performance engineers, are needed to manage the increasingly heterogeneous and diverse set of technologies. The impact of a fully digital business *ultimately drives toward the need for an adaptive architecture built on automation and fueled by data.*

Thus, business needs an architecture through which it can adapt to changing needs and requirements across all key components: data, applications, infrastructure, and security. Moreover, it needs to add architectural concepts to address the growing dependence on telemetry and automation that is enabling business to become truly digital. Business needs a digital enterprise architecture.

A Digital Enterprise Architecture Framework

In the same spirit that TOGAF and the Zachman Framework were developed— that of laying a foundation to efficiently scale business through technology—we see a need to modernize enterprise architecture with a digital framework. In a digital business, the domain distinctions of the traditional architecture remain largely intact, with notable shifts and additions:

---

21 Louis Columbus, "76% of Enterprises Prioritize AI and Machine Learning in 2021 IT Budgets," *Forbes*, January 17, 2021, *https://oreil.ly/a9tJT*; Daniel Benzaquen Moreno Nechu, "Why 85% of AI Projects Fail," *Towards Data Science*, November 11, 2020, *https://oreil.ly/romZC*.

Business

Combines key business processes, governance, company structure, and strategy into a holistic view with the goal of describing a vision of business capabilities and value to be delivered via digital services. Specifies key service-level objectives (SLOs) for digital experiences.[22]

Application delivery

Provides an overarching view of the technologies, application workloads, and interfaces required to deliver, optimize, and secure digital services.

Data

Guides development of logical and physical data models for both operational and informational data, as well as algorithms and models needed for analytics.

Technical

Specifies the network, compute, storage, and other hardware resources required to support and enable the overall architecture, but includes concepts of location (data center, cloud, and edge) as well as integrations with operations.

Operations

Describes the processes and practices necessary to operate in an increasingly autonomic environment, harnessing telemetry and automation to meet business SLOs.

Security

Provides governance over processes to ensure privacy, comply with regulations, and safeguard data. Specifies tools and technologies needed to meet policies with respect to the security of every architectural domain.

From these domains and their relationships, we can derive the digital enterprise architecture framework in Figure 1-3. The diagram illustrates how existing and new domains in an enterprise architecture intersect to address the challenges of operating as a digital business.

---

22 A service-level objective (SLO) is not the same thing as a service-level agreement (SLA), but the two are related. An *SLA* is an agreement that an application owner makes with clients or users related to performance or integrity, and an *SLO* is any performance or integrity objective that must be met to achieve an SLA.

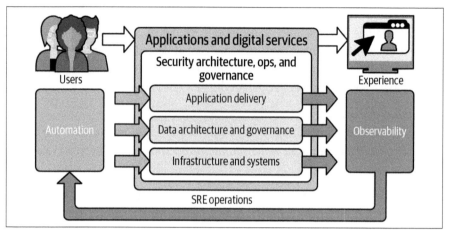

Figure 1-3. Digital enterprise architecture framework

This digital enterprise architecture describes new domains, some of which incorporate core concepts, and domains from traditional enterprise architecture:

Applications and digital services
This domain incorporates the *business* domain from traditional enterprise architecture. It transforms business entities, processes, and products into their digital complements—namely, applications and digital services. The majority (82%) of modern businesses already deliver digital services to a broad set of consumers (employees, partners, and customers).[23] As businesses continue to digitize and progress on their digital transformation journey, they will continue to expand their existing digital portfolio, and innovation will produce new lines of business and opportunities that manifest as new digital services.

Application delivery
This new domain recognizes that digital capabilities to distribute and deliver the applications, and digital services that represent business components, processes, and products, are required in a modern architecture. As business continues to become primarily digital, capabilities to ensure availability and maintain acceptable user experiences become critical to the business. These capabilities must be represented in a modern architecture. Chapter 3 explores this domain.

---

23 "The State of Application Strategy in 2022," F5, April 12, 2022, *https://oreil.ly/dlwLV*.

Data architecture and governance
Data is an integral part of the traditional enterprise architecture, and its importance to the digital business is only expanding with the inclusion of the operational data (telemetry) needed to monitor and operate digital services. This domain needs modernization as the increased volume and nature of operational data is different from traditional customer and product-related data. Both, however, benefit in a modernized enterprise architecture from the adoption of data-related operational practices and approaches that enable data mining for both business and operational insights. Data is key to enabling a digital business to adapt and innovate. Chapter 4 explores this domain.

Infrastructure and systems
The traditional *technical* domain must be updated to focus on the expanding infrastructure footprint of a digital business. The ability to operate across multiple public clouds, edge computing, and core data centers is necessary to keep digital services working at scale across the globe. This domain necessarily includes everything from hardware to operating systems and environments, incorporating models that make it possible to operate efficiently at scale. This domain is the subject of Chapter 2.

Automation and observability
A digital business relies on operational data (telemetry) to monitor the health and condition of all the components required to operate a digital service—from infrastructure, to data, to delivery and security. With every domain component generating telemetry, a digital business must be able to ingest, analyze, and act on insights to adapt in real time to conditions that threaten the user experience or the security of corporate and customer data. This domain is discussed in detail in Chapter 6.

Security architecture, ops, and governance
The role of security in enterprise architecture, like application delivery, has long been viewed as an add-on capability rather than as a full component with equal weight to other architectural domains. As you move toward a fully digital business, protecting digital assets and data becomes more critical. This is particularly true as businesses become inseparable from digital services. Security practices, tools, processes, and architecture must shift left and become a continuous practice in every domain. Chapter 5 explores this domain.

SRE operations

This domain may at first appear to be a focus on organizational change, as SRE is often viewed as a specific role rather than a domain, but *SRE operations* is more than a title or a role. According to Wikipedia *(https:// oreil.ly/scPoX)*, "Site reliability engineering is a set of principles and practices that incorporates aspects of software engineering and applies them to infrastructure and operations problems." This domain fulfills the need described by 65% of technology leaders that identified real-time digital operations as necessary to accelerating the pace of innovation in their organization.[24] SRE operations is the focus of Chapter 7.

The remainder of this book covers these domains, starting with infrastructure and systems. We then explore application delivery, then move to data, and then security. Finally, we dive into automation and observability and into SRE operations. Each chapter describes the impact of trends and changes in technology and the resulting architectural principles required to adapt and thrive in a digital-as-default age.

---

24 Vivian Chan, "New Tech Leader Survey Reveals Why the Time for Real-Time Operations Is Now," PagerDuty, November 10, 2021, *https://oreil.ly/2ozvM*.

2

An Infrastructure Renaissance

—Joel Moses, F5 CTO of Systems and distinguished engineer

For three centuries, the Renaissance drove renewed interest in classical philosophy, literature, and art. It was not the invention of the printing press by Johannes Gutenberg in 1439 that caused the Renaissance to flourish; the press was just the basic infrastructure needed for the full expression of ideas across the surface of the culture of the time. Without this infrastructure, we likely wouldn't have seen the widespread acceptance of the Copernican sciences, the austere impact of the "Ninety-five Theses" of Martin Luther, or perhaps even expeditions to the Americas. These events took place in the public consciousness born from the communication medium that Gutenberg pioneered.

The technologies of digital transformation are driving a similar rediscovery of some of the classical infrastructure elements underpinning digital businesses. Just as the advent of Gutenberg's press created new possibilities for communication for people, the emergence of newly capable infrastructure components on the internet creates new possibilities for business. As the third wave of the internet washes over the technical foundations of digital business,[1] there is renewed interest in the location, type, and capabilities of the systems that deliver compute to applications and networking.

This chapter explores the technology and standards that will impact the future of infrastructure in service of the digital business. We will explore both

---

1 Popularized by Steve Case in his 2016 book *The Third Wave* (Simon and Schuster), the third wave of the internet is occurring now, as the internet is becoming capable of embodying nearly everything—today understood as the *Internet of Things*. Preceding this third wave was the first wave, in which networking companies built the basic framework of online communications, and the second wave, in which mobile devices and the "app economy" emerged.

new mobile capabilities (5G) and container-native workloads as they drive agility into infrastructure capabilities. And we will uncover the hidden advantages of the xPU industry, which is driving unprecedented power into the edge.[2] More importantly, we will examine how organizations can take advantage of these advances in a digital enterprise architecture.

In our modern world, compute infrastructure makes up the bulk of the *technical* domain in a traditional enterprise architecture framework. Traditionally, this layer of the enterprise architecture was often designed and implemented based on the premise that workloads and users were in proximity; that is, users were located in a central corporate office with the applications they needed hosted in the data center accessible via a local area network.

But no more. Since this traditional approach to IT, we've been through three eras of application change: the internet age, the cloud computing era, and now the emergence of edge technologies and tooling. Coupled with the rapid evolution of mobile compute capabilities, this emerging era has turned on its head the premise that most application workloads are inherently "close" or "local." Users and workloads are now assumed to be both globalized from the data center and, increasingly, highly mobile.

Over four billion people—more than half the world's population—now have access to the internet. The technology is so ubiquitous that studies on internet reliance have found that 31% of adults in the US report being online "almost continuously," a measure that has risen by 21% between 2015 and 2021.[3] Similarly, mobile phones have become our constant companions. On average, Americans check their phones 344 times per day—about once every four minutes.[4]

The means by which they do so hasn't changed. Underlying infrastructure still conducts the hard work of maintaining a connection between the average 7.8 devices in the home and the apps on the internet to which they connect. What *has* changed are the demands on the user to operate the infrastructure and the requirements for software to take advantage of the services it offers. Modems and routers are now either obsolete or a commodity, with the infrastructure that

---

2 The term *xPU* refers to an entire class of specialized processing units. For further discussion, see "A Combination of Styles: The xPU" on page 33.

3 Andrew Perrin and Sara Atske, "About Three in Ten US Adults Say They Are 'Almost Constantly' Online," Pew Research Center, March 26, 2021, *https://oreil.ly/ffzz8*.

4 Trevor Wheelwright, "2022 Cell Phone Usage Statistics: How Obsessed Are We?," Reviews.org, January 24, 2022, *https://oreil.ly/ZOoBK*.

remains focused on ease of use and operation—becoming as invisible as possible to the end consumer.

The growing cohort whose lives now depend on the internet pay close attention to performance of the devices and systems that connect us. For the consumer, this typically means an ISP-provided modem, mobile devices, gaming consoles, and WiFi access points. Some consumers go to great lengths to acquire infrastructure that promises to improve performance, such as choosing a "high-performance" WiFi access point to reduce latency for online gaming or choosing the best video cards available to ensure that systems can provide the best—and fastest—graphic experience possible.

This holds true for enterprises as well. A balance of cost versus performance is always top of mind for the technology leader, especially when infrastructure is directly touching a customer-facing digital service. The impact of performance on customer satisfaction, conversion rates, and value over time is well understood. Performance is so important to the customer experience, in fact, that a staggering 73% of technology leaders would disable security controls to achieve at least a mere 1% improvement in application performance.[5]

Performance is multiplicative. Every component—from the hardware to the software to the platform to the network—contributes to either the improvement or degradation of performance. In a digital economy, your infrastructure is as important to the business as the digital services it supports. The need for infrastructure is inescapable, and the need for an improved infrastructure for digital business is unavoidable.

What Did Infrastructure Look Like Before Digital Transformation?

Put simply, infrastructure was often ignored before the digital transformation, except by members of the operations "priesthood." Infrastructure was largely hidden in the technical domain of traditional enterprise architecture.

Infrastructure has conventionally comprised all the compute, network, and storage resources necessary to deliver, scale, and secure applications and business services. Initially provisioned for use by siloed, single-function team structures with specific skill sets, this infrastructure was merely a place where applications were to land and operate—not to thrive in terms of economy, innovation, or performance. Likewise, security of applications was isolated to its own

5 "The State of Application Strategy in 2022," F5, April 12, 2022, *https://oreil.ly/KndSe*.

dedicated operations staff that created its own infrastructure to serve the need for compliance to emerging security standards.

Figure 2-1 illustrates a simplified traditional IT structure. Titles and names vary from industry to industry and from organization to organization. The common theme in these organizational structures is a tendency toward function: the organizational structure reflects specific domain expertise, such as network, data, or information security. It is not uncommon for the security team to sit outside of IT proper, under a chief information security officer (CISO) who may report to the CIO or, increasingly, to the CEO.

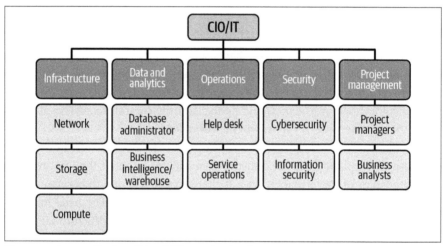

Figure 2-1. A generalized traditional IT organizational structure

This functional organizational model persists even today, with new siloed teams emerging with a focus on cloud computing. A traditional approach to IT tends toward grouping skills and expertise together. This practice leads to highly isolated, functionally based groups.

Three major evolutions have driven change into infrastructure and the IT organizational structure:

Application development began to outpace infrastructure.
Siloed teams relying on human-driven communication could not deliver the tightly coupled combination of compute, network, and storage quickly enough to satisfy the needs of the increasingly prominent application development efforts that businesses chose to undertake as part of their digital transformation. This failure led directly to the development of packaged

public cloud technologies, which afforded developers an easy way to rapidly develop.

The adoption of microservices architecture for applications is, in part, a response to these failures. Organizations that have adopted microservices architectures are seeing many benefits. Among those benefits are "faster deployment of services (69%), greater flexibility to respond to changing conditions (61%), and rapid scale of new features into large applications (56%)."[6] A key to these benefits is in the merging of infrastructure and application constructs that effectively eliminates barriers in the provisioning and operation of infrastructure inherent to traditional enterprise architectures and organizational structures.

Users became highly mobile.
The proliferation of portable computing saw a change in the primary user platform move from tethered desktops to laptops, netbooks, and, finally, an array of mobile devices including tablets and smartphones. Traditional enterprise architecture assumed that all users of applications and technology were centralized in one location, the data center. It also assumed that those users were fixed in place by the static network connections prevalent at the time. As mobility became possible after the adoption of WiFi and cellular (now 5G) technologies, traditional workstations migrated away from fixed, centralized access to mobile and decentralized devices. This magnified both the number of user accesses (many users have more than one device in active use) and the distance from an application's "center."

Attackers became more proficient at exploiting flaws in applications.
High-profile flaws in application code and libraries caused weaknesses that required more participation by more application teams in the security solution than a single-function security operations team could provide. Attack vectors have matured and expanded as the reliance on third-party components has increased; today "the average modern application contains 128 open source dependencies."[7] This does not include commercial dependencies, which tend to carry more risk as use increases because of broader availability to attackers. Security teams today must cover the entire

---

6 "Research: Microservices Bring Faster Application Delivery and Greater Flexibility to Enterprises," Tech Republic Premium, July 2, 2021, *https://oreil.ly/JmoNj*.

7 "2021 State of the Software Supply Chain," Sonatype, *https://oreil.ly/FYBHI*.

lifecycle of an application, from development to deployment to ongoing operation, as the security landscape constantly shifts and introduces risk. This requires broader skills across a variety of techniques and tools that span the entire technology stack, often referred to as *DevSecOps*, and the topic of Chapter 5.

And so, just as with the Renaissance, as new learning and technology became available, the scope of digital business likewise expanded to embrace new ideas and encounter new challenges. As mentioned, the location of data, workloads, and users is no longer centralized or fixed but includes the public cloud, edge, and endpoints. While nearly all organizations field security and delivery technologies, only one in four do so across every dimension of application distribution: in the data center, public cloud, and at the edge.[8] In the words of Southern Company CIO Martin Davis:

> *Should cloud change how IT is structured? The platforms have changed from mainframe to client server to networked to cloud over the years. Shouldn't Transformation change how IT needs to conduct business? Where IT needs to focus? And corporate business models.[9]*

The pace of change in the infrastructure domain has begun to accelerate. Let's examine some of the key changes that will impact the digital enterprise architecture of the future.

A Change in Innovation: New Standards

As noted in Chapter 1, history shows us that *standardization* always precedes periods of extreme innovation. The roads of today owe a lot of their design to the Roman chariot of old, the width of which—wheel to wheel—still defines the basic width of a modern road. Likewise, the explosive growth of the industrialization era is often attributed to the development of the assembly line, but the credit really should go to the process of standardization of parts, which made the assembly possible. In turn, manufacturers were able to focus on and propel us forward into an age of technological progress.

---

8 F5, "The State of Application Strategy in 2022."

9 Myles Suer, "Putting Together a Successful IT Organization," CMSWire, November 5, 2021, *https://oreil.ly/Rn0iV*.

AN INFRASTRUCTURE RENAISSANCE | 23

Application technology has also benefited from standardization. The communication through networking protocols that underpins the successful adoption of the internet as a digital platform came about only through creating and adhering to open standards. IP, TCP, HTTP—without these open standards, the internet as we know it would never have evolved.

Those efforts continue today with higher-order protocols that seek to standardize and improve secure communication among applications, businesses, and consumers. Those protocols once focused on enabling traditional modes of communication to work over the internet. The Session Initiation Protocol (SIP) enabled Voice over IP and served to demonstrate the capabilities of technology to replicate more human experiences. Now, most human-oriented communications—video and audio—take advantage of standardization at the application layer. The emerging metaverse seeks to merge human and digital experiences, much in the same way organizations must now merge business and technology.

So it's no surprise that organizations are focused on standardizing communications at both the infrastructure and application layers to simplify and speed the technical transition to a digital-as-default model. In planning for a digital enterprise architecture, we need to consider two broad technical trends within standards work: privacy and security standards, and edge computing standards.

PRIVACY AND SECURITY STANDARDS

It's tempting for application owners and developers to assume that standards related to privacy and security are "someone else's problem," perhaps belonging exclusively to an information security specialist or a data privacy lawyer. However, much of the responsibility for implementing controls is being placed on the application developer because of elements emerging in Web 3.0 standards. The World Wide Web Consortium (W3C) has created direct control surfaces, such as Content Security Policies, that are intended for application developers to configure in order to enhance runtime security and privacy of an application but that largely remain unconfigured and unused in practice.

Privacy is a growing concern amid the accelerated pace of digital transformation, the concerns that application users have about personal information usage, and a general reliance on data analytics for transformation tasks. Every industry is rushing to mine data, to capitalize on the increase in the use of digital devices as a primary interface to customers, suppliers, distributors, and partners. Privacy breaches have impacted every industry. As organizations progress on their digital transformation journey and become dependent on data to succeed, they must be increasingly aware of the impact of privacy concerns and seek ways to secure customer data.

When rating the importance of application services to achieving business outcomes, these security-related outcomes were singled out as very important:[10]

- Protecting customer data (65%)

- Protecting the business (52%)

- Having consistent security policies across environments (85%)

Providers face considerable pressure to offer capabilities that help customers achieve all three goals. As you work to modernize your enterprise architecture, it's important to remember that the global goal of ensuring user privacy can sometimes be at odds with your responsibility to ensure security compliance for your enterprise users. For example, using tokenization to replace user identities for protection of personally identifiable information (PII) can often impede an application owner's ability to reliably determine whether the user is a malicious bot or a human.

The most notable change that will occur in the near future is the release and forthcoming adoption of the Quick UDP Internet Connection (QUIC) transport protocol, and HTTP/3, the first application designed to run over QUIC. HTTP/3 is designed to largely replace the venerable TCP for many use cases.[11] QUIC has important performance and operational benefits, but one of the main goals in its design was to *reduce* the ability of intermediaries to observe and modify transport information by encrypting fields that the prior protocols leave open.

The fight against pervasive user activity monitoring remains a major priority at the Internet Engineering Task Force (IETF) and sometimes counters the short-term interests of both service providers and enterprises by reducing monitoring and management capabilities. While end-user privacy is a first-order principle for many stakeholders, it can sometimes increase the attack surface of application flows by eliminating the ability to see inside them.

Obviously, massive numbers of applications are built atop HTTP, and an update to the standard affects many of them. QUIC is here to stay: Meta, Google, Microsoft, Apple, Mozilla Corporation, Akamai Technologies, Fastly, F5, and

---

10 "The State of Application Strategy 2021," F5, *https://oreil.ly/5r1h9.*

11 "QUIC in the Internet Industry," IETF, June 3, 2021, *https://oreil.ly/OgLhz*; AsyncBanana, "What Is HTTP/3 and Why Does It Matter?," JavaScript in Plain English, May 9, 2021, *https://oreil.ly/EJzrw.*

Cloudflare are all investing heavily in HTTP/3 on both the client and server side. As we saw with other protocol standards originally proposed by Google (and popularized via its dominant position in the browser market), wider adoption appears inevitable. This change, in combination with other privacy-enhancing tools, like DNS over HTTPS (DoH), continues to deploy across the internet.

THE CHALLENGE TO VISIBILITY AND HOW TO OVERCOME IT

Although all these changes have many benefits for applications and end users, they require upgrades and complicate the ability of operators to measure, manage, and secure their infrastructure. Traditional infrastructure architecture was built on the assumption that intermediaries such as switches, proxies, and security devices could inspect traffic and evaluate application payloads. With the adoption of QUIC, this will no longer be a safe assumption. As a digital business needs visibility into every system, down to the network, the loss of capabilities to inspect and examine data flowing across the network will be felt by business and technical stakeholders alike.

Lack of visibility already frustrates stakeholders in their quest to uncover the root cause of outages and application performance degradations. Incomplete visibility leaves a digital business blind to possible attacks. For technology leaders, a lack of visibility also makes it difficult to align SLOs with business outcomes related to customer experience. Chapter 6 explores this topic in greater depth.

Enterprises will need to consider the change in visibility and plan for the inclusion of monitoring capabilities within a digital enterprise architecture. Native, or built-in, instrumentation of every system is currently the best option to ensure full visibility across all architectural layers. This is particularly true for organizations embracing the use of infrastructure across multiple environments, such as the public cloud, colocation centers, and edge platforms.

Standardizing monitoring capabilities—including the format of telemetry data—will be your best option to achieve the visibility needed. OpenTelemetry (OTEL) is the leading standard in the effort to accomplish this task. As the Cloud Native Computing Foundation (CNCF) puts it, OTEL is "a collection of tools, APIs, and SDKs. Use it to instrument, generate, collect, and export telemetry data (metrics, logs, and traces) to help you analyze your software's performance and behavior."[12] It is currently the most popular observability standard, with

---

12 CNCF, OpenTelemetry website, accessed May 29, 2022, https://oreil.ly/NWcKx.

more than half (54%) of organizations adopting its use to normalize how operational data is generated.[13]

A more open, standards-based approach to monitoring infrastructure moves organizations away from traditional agent-based—and often functionally siloed—systems and enables the collection of operational data in a centralized data lake. Access to a consolidated data store enables businesses to analyze and mine for insights and more accurately forecast capacity and demand. These capabilities are beneficial to organizations in understanding the health and status of the infrastructure underpinning digital services.

EDGE COMPUTE STANDARDS

The success of the internet as a platform for business is largely due to the interoperability achieved by standardizing network and communications protocols. This standardization means that we have not only stable ways to communicate but also emerging ways to compute in a standardized way.

The emerging edge offers even greater expansion and the ability to address the long-term obstacles imposed by the laws of physics on performance. Standardization of application and transport protocols will enable the portability that businesses need in order to take advantage of extending their infrastructure layer to diverse locations. Further standardization of compute environments will then deliver the capability to run workloads closer to the user than ever before.

Consider, if you will, an application that performs facial and object recognition built atop a generative-adversarial-network-based (GAN-based) AI learning model. Two compute needs must be satisfied for this use case: a place for learning new faces and objects, and a place to process the learning model to discover those faces and objects. Sophisticated AI learning mechanisms are compute intensive and often outstrip the capacity of whole data centers, let alone the system at the edge feeding it video data. But model training doesn't necessarily generate real-time feedback; instead, its learning is done iteratively and typically provided back to the application as a packaged runtime. The actual *processing* of the AI model for this use case does typically require real-time feedback toward the system hosting the sensor, however. Can you imagine a facial-recognition sensor attached to a door lock that requires video to be sent to a data center hundreds of miles away for a decision to unlock? No, that AI model processing

---

13 Alex Woodie, "Companies Drowning in Observability Data," Datanami, January 20, 2022, https://oreil.ly/GECYV.

can—and should—be done most effectively at the edge (which, in this case, is next to the camera and the lock that it serves).

Analysts predict that the leading cloud service providers will have a distributed ATM-like presence to serve a subset of their services for low-latency application requirements.[14] Many cloud service providers are already investing in ways to make their services available closer (*https://oreil.ly/Myi7E*) to the users who need to access them. This trend will continue as the granularity of the regions covered by these cloud service providers increases. *Micro data centers* will be in areas where a high population of users congregates, while *pop-up* cloud service points will support temporary requirements like sporting events and concerts.

To take advantage of this, either organizations need to employ teams with new skills or the market needs to provide a way for them to transparently deploy applications and services at the edge by using resources that may or may not be native to the app or service.

WebAssembly (Wasm) is an emerging standard undertaken by the W3C that will likely underpin the "close" execution of application workloads to mobile users for enterprise applications. Wasm exists in every browser currently made and is emerging as a popular way to render server-side application workloads. For example, Google is already using Wasm to craft native application experiences for classical applications like Google Maps.

Wasm is important because it is a platform-agnostic way of executing application code. A binary compiled for Wasm can be written in any language and executed on a variety of platform types. It becomes possible for a developer to write an application in their favorite language, compile it once, and run it both on an enterprise server and an Internet of Things (IoT) device. This true portability allows application code to become part of adaptability because its execution is not bound to a particular type of compute. You will see how this flexibility becomes especially important to our digital enterprise architecture in a moment.

A Change in Focus: Density and Economy

The siloed data centers of the past dealt with a limited number of applications distributed to a small number of users in fixed locations. These applications ran largely on handcrafted infrastructure components chosen mainly for their

---

14 Meghan Rimol, "4 Trends Impacting Cloud Adoption in 2020," Gartner, May 29, 2020, *https://oreil.ly/pG4Sd*.

reliability, and secondarily for their performance. It did not matter whether the application infrastructure or runtime was in any way *efficient* or *compact*. As such, the data centers of the age became power hungry and space starved to such a degree that the adoption of the public cloud was viewed as not only a faster way to instantiate infrastructure but also a way to reduce the power and cooling bills of an organization.

But things have now changed, and this requires us to rethink the use of infrastructure to fit new technologies and standards. The future now suggests a massive number of widely distributed applications to large numbers of highly mobile users. What characteristics do we now seek for our digital enterprise architecture? The sheer number of distributed instances and users facing us—combined with new capabilities afforded us by the adoption of new standards—suggests that we refocus on efficiency and cost. Luckily, an emerging wave of infrastructure allows us to target these ratio-changers without sacrificing performance or reliability.

AN ARMS RACE

It may surprise you to know that part of the way the industry is responding to the shift in location and density we've mentioned is based on mobile computing and is (probably) already in your pocket. If you carry an iPhone or use a newer Macintosh, you've encountered an ARM processor. *ARM* is a type of processor architecture that competes directly with the established instruction set architecture (ISA) that most CPUs and applications use: Intel x86. ARM processors are in many mobile devices and are aggressively appearing in compute infrastructure related to networking (more on that later).

Developed by the United Kingdom–based home computer manufacturer Acorn Computers in 1985, the ARM processor used a type of instruction set that was focused less on general functionality and more on efficiency of execution: reduced instruction set computer (RISC). The resulting invention, called the *Acorn RISC Machine*, became commonly known simply as ARM.[15] Furthermore, this processor design was created as an openly communicated standard, relatively unencumbered by licensing. ARM licenses are far less expensive than other architectures (save for RISC-V), and can be obtained by vendors holistically, allowing them to produce their own silicon designs based on the architecture. Apple has done so with its M-series processors, as has Amazon.

---

15 Some refer to *ARM* as the "Advanced RISC Machine," but those people are probably more concerned with trademarks than actual history.

While other chip ISA variants have come and mostly gone over the last several decades, today's CPU market has come to be dominated by these two architectures. Many companies have built their business models and software around the x86 ISA and have to date mostly ignored ARM. However, the rise of distributed cloud and edge architectures is seeing a renewed interest in the efficiency afforded by a RISC processor architecture.

The role of performance in ARM's success

Efficiency alone is not the only reason a transition is underway. With the RISC model being adopted by large-scale design partners (notably Apple), successive generations of ARM core design have now closed the traditional performance gap that these processors have had versus the Intel x86. ARM cores are, gigahertz to gigahertz, no longer inferior to x86 chips. The advancement in foundry capabilities by Taiwan Semiconductor Manufacturing Company (TSMC) and Samsung has enabled ARM processor transistor density, performance, and performance per watt to surpass that of the x86.

The consumption of ARM processor cores within traditional infrastructure has also significantly changed through vertically integrated hyperscale companies, including public clouds. Several of these companies have elected to no longer pay silicon vendors to produce CPUs but are instead designing their own devices utilizing the ARM standard. By keeping these designs in house and using the silicon foundries only for manufacturing, they now have control of design trade-offs, the supply chain, and cost structures of the CPU devices that underpin their compute infrastructure. In the past few years, Apple's M1, Amazon's Nitro and Graviton, and NVIDIA's Grace processors have marked a shift from the traditional CPU suppliers to in-house silicon. We expect this momentum will continue onward to Microsoft, Google, Meta, and others.

Implications for the market

How much is this transition likely to affect the market? Figure 2-2 shows the projected market share impact of these new realities on the x86 as compared to the ARM competition (as forecast by SoftBank). It suggests a ~20% growth of ARM-based CPUs within cloud environments by 2028. Given recent changes in ARM adoption, growth is likely to occur even faster than this.

As with Wasm, we can use the new capabilities of ARM to address the flexibility needed to improve the organization's ability to adapt to changing needs with efficient use of this emerging platform type. Selection of a development process and language framework that is efficient on both x86 and ARM is an excellent way to accomplish this. Likewise, the software ecosystem barriers that formerly plagued adoption of ARM have largely disappeared. Linux distributions now universally support ARM cpus, and platform-as-a-service (PaaS) vendors like Red Hat (OpenShift) and VMware (ESXi) have completed the work to run atop ARM.

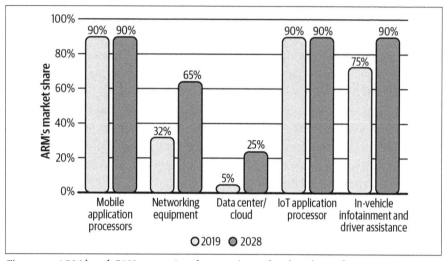

Figure 2-2. ARM-based CPUs are projected to grow in market share by 2028

ADVANTAGES FOR A DIGITAL BUSINESS

To understand the advantages of ARM, let's look at Amazon Web Services (AWS), which is leading the way in public cloud ARM adoption with its Graviton CPU. Nodes built with this Amazon-designed, ARM-based CPU are being made available directly to customers as rentable Amazon Elastic Compute Cloud (EC2) instances as well as indirectly by hosting AWS infrastructure and services. These customers are effectively seeking for themselves what you are seeking for your digital enterprise architecture: higher adaptability and freedom to innovate. They're attempting to gain both in two areas: density of provisionable compute and lower cost of operation.

Both sets of goals are shared by CIOs and technology leaders everywhere, and it is no surprise that the lower cost of operations achieved by public cloud providers has been a compelling reason for organizations to embrace the public cloud.

Changes in the efficiency and performance of CPUs available to the enterprise market will net improvements in capacity, especially when coupled with the use of virtualization or container technologies that increase the density of a provisionable compute. The movement of as-a-service workloads onto less expensive ARM nodes therefore presents a clear opportunity and risk as you are modernizing your infrastructure. Those able to quickly pivot into the new, lower-cost ARM environment will flourish, while those left behind on the x86 infrastructure will struggle.

One might think that the benefits of ARM-based performance and cost service engineering are only for the hyperscale provider, but the emergence of the xPU space is bringing this capability into the arms of the enterprise.

A Change in Capability: The xPU Wave

As we touched on in the introduction, the traditional building blocks of infrastructure have largely been commoditized or turned into software components on general-purpose compute. The efficiency of this infrastructure, however, has slowly been decreasing as workloads grow more complex, while expectations of performance continue to expand.

Fear is growing that we are nearing an artificial horizon to the infrastructure's growth: the slow but steady death of Moore's law. In 1965, Gordon Moore, cofounder of Fairchild Semiconductor (*https://oreil.ly/Gla57*) and Intel (*https://oreil.ly/EclfT*), unintentionally established a technology axiom known today as *Moore's law*. His prediction that the number of components per integrated circuit would double every year held true for nearly half a century. Moore's law posits that compute power will increase as technology finds new ways to deliver the things needed to support it: a new fabrication method, new materials, or tighter processes have helped deliver on that prediction well.

But that's not enough for those who believe that the emerging problems sets we face—AI, quantum-safe cryptography, and meeting ever-increasing threats to applications—will require us to discard this traditional view of general-purpose compute. As Dave Vellante and David Floyer observe, "The outcome of Moore's law was that performance would double every 24 months, or about 40% annually. CPU performance improvements have now slowed to roughly 30% annually."[16]

Technology leaders typically refresh hardware resources on a well-defined schedule, averaging every two to five years. For an enterprise about to begin

---

16 Dave Vellante and David Floyer, "A New Era of Innovation: Moore's Law Is Not Dead and AI Is Ready to Explode," *SiliconANGLE*, April 10, 2021, *https://oreil.ly/KYZQp*.

efforts to modernize infrastructure as a prelude to more expansive efforts to enable a digital business, the benefit of such a refresh in the face of declining improvements in performance and capacity appear minimal.

The good news for technology leaders is that we *could* read this to mean that Moore's law is only *technically* dead. As has been noted by many industry watchers, if Moore's law is expanded to include the growing subset of *specialized processing units*, performance is improving at rates of greater than 100% annually. Let's talk for a moment about the difference between general-purpose and specialized compute, as this is one of the ways in which infrastructure can be modernized to meet the needs of a fully digital business.

COMPUTE STYLES

The traditional complex instruction set computer (CISC) processor we have all traditionally used is built primarily to satisfy a broad and generic set of computing problems. Over time, CISC processors like x86 have gained new capabilities like floating-point math, predictive branching, and more—all aimed at producing a balanced outcome of the larger set of application tasks to which the processor may be applied. But this balance comes at a cost:

- Additional complexity, because added logic to detect and apply optimizations is needed.

- Scaling back the performance of a processor feature so the performance of another will not "starve."

- As a result, the processor spends a substantial amount of electrical energy.

The result, in general-purpose compute, is a solution that's correct but may have taken a circuitous path. The solution to some of these performance and power costs comes in two distinct modes of specialized compute: domain-specific compute and the transparent assist compute processor.

Domain-specific compute

Domain-specific compute is a type of hardware processing that derives its performance and efficiency gains from specifically tailoring the problem to be solved to the compute capability that is available. The most visible example of this is in the field of AI, where it has become popular to use graphics processing units (GPUs) to perform the complex mathematical inferencing that underpins some of the analysis that must be done. It was discovered that a GPU, whose strength is in using a large number of parallel math cores (arithmetic logic units, or ALUs) to compute vectors, was exceptionally good at using those same cores for a different purpose than graphical display. The only thing that was needed was a proper division of the problem set into something that the GPU could compute.

Transparent assistive compute

That's where *transparent assistive compute* emerges. It's seen mostly in communication technologies used on compute hosts, such as the network interface card (NIC). Because the computational cycles involved in formatting messages for delivery over the network are repetitive and standard, compute vendors started adding assistive logic to these cards for certain elements that formerly required multiple trips through a host's general-purpose processor to complete.

This type of processing offload has grown to include data transport, security, and network functions—none of which requires software modifications to use. These feature-heavy NICs are now known as *smart NICs* to distinguish them from their simpler predecessors. A common thread of all the smart NIC features is that they represent the offload of noncore functionality that an application needs but that is outside the business logic of the application itself.

A COMBINATION OF STYLES: THE XPU

Taking lessons from both domain-specific compute and transparent assistive compute, a new class of infrastructure is now emerging that holds great promise for digital enterprise architecture: the *xPU*. Unlike traditional processing unit designations, which reference a specific type of processor with a narrowly defined domain of execution, an xPU is "a complete cross-architecture computing solution across all major chip types, all tied together in a single application programming interface, assigning each task to whichever chip is best suited to process it."[17]

One of the first tangible instances of an xPU is a data processing unit (DPU). The DPU combines several processor types into a single unit with the goal of moving data very quickly. To achieve this, the DPU leaves behind the limited offload-only smart NIC and likewise dispenses with the idea of being a dependent part of its host server. It aspires instead to be its own server class system capable of hosting full-fledged, heavyweight software components.

A typical DPU is a single-unit, standalone bootable computer system that attaches inside another compute host. Such a compute node affords the

---

17 Francoise von Trapp, "What Is an xPU and Where Can I Get One?," *3D InCites*, April 15, 2021, https://oreil.ly/LdbbM.

possibility of running entirely self-contained services along the communications channel, as illustrated in Figure 2-3. A DPU provides the benefits of a cloud provider's division-of-services infrastructure discussed in the previous section, without the need to create and maintain custom compute for this purpose within an enterprise. It merely becomes a provisionable location on each host, where the work of application delivery and security can be easily performed.

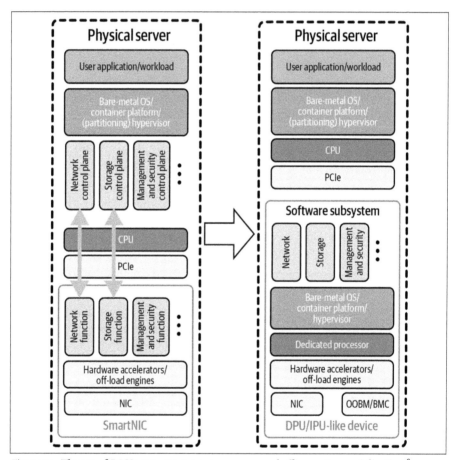

Figure 2-3. The use of DPU separates compute concerns and offers greater specialization[18]

The DPU is disruptive because it creates a new and highly capable location for the insertion of many application delivery, security, and network functions.

---

18 In the figure, OOBM stands for "out-of-band management" (*https://oreil.ly/TQ1yI*); BMC stands for "baseboard management controller" (*https://oreil.ly/VMpjC*).

It is clearly different from the historical insertion points of a physical appliance, a separate COTS node, or a same-node sidecar. This hardware instead allows application services to be deployed in the host server (the box), while not actually running on the host CPU and taking performance away from application compute. It also has the advantage of not needing independent rack space as an appliance would, not requiring additional COTS nodes, and not consuming host node resources (cores, memory, storage). And at predicted market prices, each node is likely to be substantially less expensive than the historical alternatives, making possible a universal deployment across the entire compute infrastructure, as AWS has done with the Graviton2 processor.

Within a few years, this technology will be nearly ubiquitous, allowing enterprises for the first time to achieve (provided the right software stack) the cost and performance benefits that Amazon has achieved with its internal ARM adoption for infrastructure.

These cost efficiencies alone are not enough to entice enterprises to completely abandon the public cloud. But when coupled with more efficient operational models, such as SRE approaches, the benefits become nearly impossible to ignore. When services and telemetry collection are built into a resilient layer ahead of the application, SRE operation tasks become far more reliable and do not conflict with the compute serving the application. The relationship between SRE approaches and adaptability are more fully explored in Chapter 7. Suffice it to say here that significantly strong correlations exist between the adoption of SRE operations and repatriation from the public cloud. Organizations that rely on SRE operations are nearly 10 times more likely to repatriate.[19] When added to the financial gains from a transition to ARM and DPU hardware in the enterprise, the benefits of repatriation—demonstrated by Sarah Wang (*https://oreil.ly/1KM96*) and Martin Casado (*https://oreil.ly/qkC4m*) in "The Cost of a Cloud: A Trillion Dollar Paradox" (*https://oreil.ly/Qfa6P*)—will be difficult to ignore.

Conclusion

No one predicted that the simple invention of a simple machine that applied ink to paper would unleash the greatest wave of change that the world has ever seen. A Renaissance is a time of intense upheaval, when commonly held beliefs are challenged, and a time of incredible uncertainty. It is a time when the pace of creativity often exceeds understanding.

---

19 F5, "The State of Application Strategy in 2022."

Technology leaders face a moment in the transformation to a digital enterprise architecture in which they must build an infrastructure that can support the applications and digital services that businesses will need not just to survive but to thrive in a digital economy. There are, indeed, powerful market trends driving toward a new emergence of leading-edge infrastructure. These include workload repatriation from the public cloud, the need for distribution of applications to the edge, industrial IoT enterprises, and an urgent need to secure application data and access from cyber attackers.

At the same time, seismic shifts are occurring in what infrastructure is and what it can do. Between emerging standards, the shift to ARM-based architectures, and the rise of assistive compute in the advent of the DPU, we must all find our path through the uncertainty and upheaval. We can either ride these trends—and see them become the centerpiece of a new infrastructure architecture—or allow them to swamp us. The dedicated pursuit of a better adaptability ratio—one that shifts infrastructure workloads and application services off the host nodes, into cross-platform containers, and onto DPUs with superior security—will win the day. Companies that can facilitate this architecture, and adopt application services leveraging it, will see significant financial rewards and opportunities. Those that ignore this disruptive change will see diminished opportunities as the data-center architecture evolves away from their applications.

3

From Marathon to Messaging

—Lori MacVittie, F5 principal technical evangelist

The noted Greek historian Plutarch introduced the world to the phrase "marathon run" in a tale of Philippides and his legendary race to deliver a message to the Greek Assembly. Philippides ran approximately 25 miles, from Marathon to Athens, to inform the Greek Assembly of victory in the Battle of Marathon (*https://oreil.ly/26tTp*). The story became legendary because of his dedication to his task. Not only did he shed his clothing to improve his speed on his run, but he promptly fell dead after delivering his message. The distance became known as a "marathon" in honor of his efforts and has been immortalized by many historians and writers throughout history.

Humans have constantly evolved and improved the methods by which we deliver information, both in terms of speed and security. From the Pony Express and postal services to email and instant messaging, technology has helped to evolve the way we communicate. But the form of these methods has remained largely the same: they are based on intermediaries—whether people or technology—to carry a message between two endpoints.

Conway's law tells us that "organizations design systems that mirror their own communication structure."[1] This is true, even when those organizations are as large as societies. Consider how technology mirrors the delivery and receipt of secured communications. You can take a letter to the post office and ask that it be delivered only to a specific person, with proof made via a signature. In digital terms, this is reflected in requiring client-side certificates to authenticate the receiver of a message. Similar functions exist around secure protocols like

---

1 "Conway's law," Wikipedia, accessed June 8, 2022, *https://oreil.ly/KaleW*.

Secure Shell (SSH), which establishes the digital identity of two endpoints and encrypts all communication occurring over a subsequent connection.

The functions responsible for handling and securing digital messages are collectively known as *app delivery* and *security*. Traditional enterprise architecture was designed without these functions, largely because the emergence of app delivery as a class of capabilities occurred long after organizations standardized on an architecture framework.

These functions either did not exist or were not seen as critical until the widespread use of the internet. But they have become integral to every digital service, and their evolution can be understood by exploring how technology mirrors changes in human communication.

Human and Digital Communications

Applications are the primary means by which businesses engage with—and retain—customers today. Convenience and performance are the criteria that consumers use to judge a brand, regardless of industry. The number of users and engagement metrics for an app are considered on par with financial assets. This is leading to highly competitive markets in which the time to realize value through applications is critical to business success. Pressure from the market to deliver, in turn, is driving internal urgency to develop, deploy, and deliver faster and more frequently.

Traditional IT cannot meet these demands. Operational efficiencies are required if IT is to deliver faster time to value. Over half (65%) of those in DevOps roles have admitted that lack of access to the deployment pipeline has driven them to "go around" IT and use the public cloud instead.[2]

The pressure to improve the delivery of software is driving the adoption of emerging technologies faster than ever before. Nearly one in five developers (19%) were *already employing* serverless computing at the end of 2017.[3] In late 2021, 68% either had adopted or planned to adopt serverless by 2023.[4] Container usage is already nearing mainstream adoption.

---

2 "NetOps Meets DevOps: The State of Network Automation," F5 and Red Hat, 2018, *https://oreil.ly/munOZ*.

3 "The 14th Annual State of the Developer Nation," Developer Economics, March 19, 2018, *https://oreil.ly/PYmUg*.

4 "Serverless in the Enterprise," IBM, 2021, *https://oreil.ly/bLmeE*.

Yet the death of mainframes and monoliths has been greatly exaggerated. Many of these transactional applications, built before the internet could support processing at scale with the security required to protect sensitive data, continue —and will continue—to operate for many reasons, including capacity and speed. They are part of a larger category of applications we generally group together as *traditional* applications, to distinguish them from *modern* applications. The distinction is important, as you will soon see.

TRADITIONAL APPLICATIONS

In the early 1980s, when computing became an integral part of business functions, it was obvious that security and skill sets demanded a way for a broader set of users to access these applications. New application architectures emerged to address that need, leading to a surge in client/server applications.

When the internet emerged and businesses began to extend their reach to the World Wide Web, yet another class of applications arose to leverage new network and infrastructure capabilities: three-tier web applications.

Yet all three architectures share a key characteristic: they are *transactional*. This is not only because of technical limitations of the time, but also because early digitization practices merely viewed applications as digital manifestations of manual, paper-based processes.

Transactional is best understood by the "fill out this form and submit it" paradigm that dominated much of the 20th century. Nearly all processes followed this communication pattern, which is modeled after our human patterns.

Conway's Law in Action

Consider that the predominant form of communication in the 20th century was still letters. Email transformed only the *delivery* of the communication. Email was—and often still is—a full-length letter. The way in which we communicated was both constrained and shaped by the technology available at the time to package and deliver communications. Even as delivery shifted toward digital, our use of that technology remained strongly tied to the way in which we communicated via letter.

Even the advent of the automated teller machine (ATM) did not break out of the transactional paradigm. For all its buttons and modern appearances, ATMs still collected a required set of information and then—and only then—did it dial up the bank and submit it.

Thus, the defining characteristic of traditional applications is their *transactional* nature. Essentially, communications, regardless of application architecture, are assumed to represent a transaction. This, in turn, dictates the design of user interfaces. Web forms, service registration, and data entry screens are examples of transaction-driven design.

It should be noted that the operational model of traditional applications was also transactional. An entire application package, from platforms to delivery, was updated in a single event, much in the same way data was exchanged between components.

The impact of a transactional operational model on business and IT rhythms is seen in tightly controlled release and maintenance windows along with scheduled downtime. It is also seen in the predominant software development methodology of the time: waterfall. The process was linear and highly transactional, with each phase of the lifecycle having well-defined beginnings and endings.

MODERN APPLICATIONS

Cloud computing emerged about the same time that mobile phones became capable of running applications. The sudden need to support mobile (untethered) users with limited processing power shifted assumptions about the way applications collected and exchanged data. Smaller, more frequent exchanges became desirable and, because of the increasing availability of broadband and more powerful wireless communications, feasible.

Mobile also introduced us to a less traditional model of correspondence: text. While instant messaging had been available via the web for some time, the notion of *interactive* digital conversations did not really gain momentum until mobile communications introduced us to the text message. Suddenly, our communication became iterative and more accurately represented a conversation rather than an exchange of information as it had with letters and email.

The traditional transactional (asynchronous) model, which required a "complete form," was not compatible with this new paradigm. An interstitial architecture began to form to compensate. Temporary data storage (sessions) arose on both client- and server-side applications that enabled user interfaces to become more interactive. Data was saved in sessions over time and, finally, submitted to a transactional system in one big "form."

Conway's Law in Action

It's no coincidence that "data suggests the ideal length of an email is between 50 and 125 words."[5] Modern technology such as text and media platforms support shorter, more synchronous exchanges, effectively building out a complete—and asynchronous—conversation in short bursts. This digital model more closely resembles a face-to-face conversation and is preferred by most over email when information is time sensitive.[6]

These iterative data exchanges gave rise to Web 2.0, an evolutionary step forward for the three-tier architecture. Like mobile apps, they were made possible by API-driven development. APIs enabled developers to provide a way to collect smaller chunks of data associated with a specific business entity such as a product or service. Eventually, the process concluded by aggregating that data into a single transaction for execution by a traditional application.

But as organizations began to leverage the cloud to deliver a growing portfolio of consumer-facing applications, the fragility of this patched-together model became evident. Connectivity disruptions caused the loss of temporary data stored in sessions, and the need to share that data across systems was incompatible with the growing adoption of stateless architectural design.

Frustrated by the inability of traditional architectures to address the need for frequent releases, updates, and patches in a cloud operational model, developers introduced a new application architecture that integrated a more agile operational model: microservices. The clear separation of components in a microservices architecture also enabled targeted updates and patches. But even as developers became proficient in updating only parts of their application and adopted a more agile method of developing software, IT was not ready to support this new model.

Microservices solved the problem of trying to map entity-based data-collection APIs to transactional systems. The use of APIs more closely mirrors an interactive conversation between participants instead of the traditional, transactional exchange of bulk data. Now, systems were designed to model business

---

5 Mike Renahan, "The Ideal Length of a Sales Email, Based on 40 Million Emails," HubSpot, October 19, 2018, *https://oreil.ly/mIZ8J*.

6 Jacklyn Kellick, "58 Percent of Consumers Say That Texting Is the Best Way for Businesses to Reach Them Quickly," Business Wire, February 9, 2021, *https://oreil.ly/9NKwc*.

entities, with APIs available to facilitate the exchange of the data the system governed. This change allowed mobile and web-based applications to leverage their own local storage and offered the interactivity expected by increasingly digital-native consumers.

Additionally, localizing workloads enabled an *incremental* operational model that supports targeted updates and scale. An incremental operational model coupled with microservices is ultimately more efficient and enables frequent updates and patches needed to respond to consumer demands and a constantly evolving threat landscape.

The impact of an incremental operational model on business and IT rhythms is seen in the transparent, frequent updates that no longer require scheduled downtime or maintenance windows. Changes to configuration and policies are now incremental and happen on a much more frequent basis. Much of this is enabled by an approach that treats infrastructure as code and brings together automation and Agile practices. Agile practices are central to the cultural change needed to transition from a transactional model to an iterative one that supports changes in the frequency with which apps and services are delivered in a digital business.

The Role of App Delivery

The communication structures that humans rely on are increasingly based on technology; in other words, they are digital. This can be seen by digital communications' impact on the economy. Research predicts that by the end of 2022, 65% of global gross domestic product (GDP) will be digitalized.[7]

The coupling of the economy to digital services means they are fast approaching the status of *necessary infrastructure*. Like the infrastructure that enables the delivery of physical communications, the digital "information highway" must be reliable and secure. That highway comprises networks and infrastructure that span data centers, cloud providers, and increasingly, edge environments. Furthermore, the distribution of applications across core, cloud, and edge, coupled with the shift toward microservices architectures, amplifies the number and location of workloads in need of delivery and security. These technologies can no longer be ad hoc functionality bolted onto workloads but must be deliberately deployed based on business needs and desired outcomes.

---

7 "Global Interconnection Index: Volume 5," Equinix, 2021, *https://oreil.ly/OqraL*.

Thus, it is no surprise that this results in the "need for a digital infrastructure optimized for proximity to, and interconnection with, networks and clouds."[8]

App delivery and security technologies are concerned with issues of availability, performance, and security of applications. From the earliest days of load balancing to today's advanced and AI-driven anti-fraud and anti-abuse services, these functions have grown in importance as digital services have become a societal staple.

Traditionally, the details of message delivery and security have been left to a proxy—and by extension, to the people who operate these intermediaries (typically, network administrators). But the rapid pace of technical innovation now affords developers and operators, and the business itself, the ability to dictate speed and monitor progress of message delivery. This requires a shift to a more collaborative approach to application delivery that's inclusive of developers and operators, as well as a decoupling of app delivery from the technical (networking and infrastructure) domain, to liberate these functions from being restrained by policies and processes that do not directly serve the needs of applications.

Conway's Law in Action

This need for observability, i.e., visibility into every step and system involved, again transfers from the human realm to that of the digital. We expect visibility into the delivery of our packages and communications. We are informed when our text messages are delivered, and updated on the location of an incoming package. Our technology mirrors the way we communicate, and so we see increasing demand for data to inform stakeholders about every step in delivering digital services. This operational data comes from every layer of the enterprise architecture and is a critical part of the enterprise architecture that will be more fully explored in Chapter 4. For app delivery and security, the ability to produce and subsequently act on operational data collected across systems and environments is crucial to the ability of businesses to act in real time to meet customer expectations regarding delivery.

8 "Global Interconnection Index: Volume 4," Equinix, *https://oreil.ly/S3iuw.*

These systems are integral to digital services. Whether DNS or load balancing for scale, whether anti-fraud and anti-abuse or API protection services, app delivery and security technologies are an indispensable technology today to ensure security, optimize performance, and maintain availability of digital services.

Today, these functions are not only in use but a necessary part of a scalable, secure digital business. Moreover, the broad adoption of cloud computing and the emergence of a robust edge ecosystem put pressure on app delivery to include a growing number of elements and environments that are not represented by existing architecture frameworks. As Yoshimasa Masuda and Murlikrishna Viswanathan explain in *Enterprise Architecture for Global Companies in a Digital IT Era* (Springer), more recent technologies such as mobile and cloud computing have no representation in traditional architecture models. This is also true for app delivery.

The evolution of app delivery into a discipline of its own, fully represented in an enterprise architecture, is necessary to enable digital business. The app delivery discipline combines tools and technologies with operational practices to ensure digital services meet SLOs for scalability, performance, and reliability (a topic we dig into in Chapter 7):

- Tools and technologies include DNS, load balancing, API gateways, ingress control, and service mesh.

- Key capabilities include observability and the ability to be harnessed to automation toolchains.

- Key operational practices comprise application monitoring, automated SLO thresholding and alerting, and well-defined operational response plans.

The process of elevating app delivery out of the traditional technical domain and into its own mirrors that of the abstractions inherent in the network stack —the Open Systems Interconnection (OSI) model—on which modern digital technologies rely. That model assumes that for each layer, the layers beneath it are present and reliable. For example, modern delivery services that focus on securing or scaling applications operate at the application layer of the OSI stack. That is, they focus on HTTP-related functions and assume that connectivity (TCP) and networking (IP) are reliable and handled by other infrastructure. In this way, services such as load balancing, caching, and application security have decoupled themselves from the technical infrastructure. Without being bound to a specific technical layer, these services have increasingly dispersed, leading to new deployment locations and models. This includes the growing adoption of "as a service" models, in which security and acceleration services reside outside the enterprise domain.

This model is also seen in the broad use of cloud computing, in which application-oriented services are often deployed as a service either as part of the cloud-provider ecosystem or individually from third-party providers.

In both cases, app delivery and security services exist outside the traditional technical domain and are not bound by network and infrastructure policies and guidelines. This makes it difficult to make the appropriate choices necessary to measure efficacy of desired business outcomes, optimize costs, or contribute to the business. Technically, this results in a lack of consistency that leaves organizations vulnerable to attack and unable to respond to performance degradations or outages. To wit, 44% of organizations cite the inability to consistently apply security to all applications as a challenge when operating in multicloud environments.[9]

The Impact on Adaptability

Adaptability depends on the balance between those maintaining the core and those innovating. This equation is universally true across the organization. IT functions, regardless of domain, are particularly susceptible to the law of diminishing returns: adding more resources to address the challenge of improving velocity and efficacy has the *opposite* effect, compounding delays by introducing new communication layers, adding overhead, and increasing opportunities for misunderstandings and mistakes.[10] The effect of adding more resources is combinatorial, which makes it particularly detrimental to the ability of an organization to adapt, as time spent on communications is considered a core function, not innovation.

The result is an impact on the cost of doing business. Time spent focusing on identifying the source of incidents consumes both time and money. An average of $1.7 million per organization in lost productivity is attributed to the 16% of time spent by IT meeting with business stakeholders to identify the causes of and solutions to problems.[11]

---

9 "The State of Application Strategy in 2022," F5, April 12, 2022, *https://oreil.ly/9kpOA*.

10 Frederick P. Brooks, Jr., *The Mythical Man-Month* (Boston: Addison-Wesley, 1995).

11 "Global CIO Report," Dynatrace, 2021, *https://oreil.ly/v1nkO*.

Further reducing the efficacy of operations with respect to app delivery is the distribution of apps and services across cloud, core, and edge locations. As noted in Chapter 2, existing tools and processes were designed for a traditional framework like TOGAF based on well-known, hardwired, static connections. A modern architecture framework needs to manage dynamic, on-demand, temporary connections because of the current mobility of users and the increasing mobility of workloads across locations and global regions.

This mobility has a profound impact on app delivery, effectively decoupling it from the infrastructure and establishing it as a layer of protection and services that operate as intermediaries to applications. These services are deployed in such a way as to execute specific capabilities on behalf of an application. As application portfolios disperse, the app security and delivery services that provide these capabilities also disperse and now reside in all environments, from core to cloud to edge to the endpoint. As of 2022, the typical enterprise operates an average of 14 different app security and delivery services at its core (on premises) and 11 in the public cloud.[12]

Any single application—whether it is a traditional monolith or has a modern, microservices-based architecture—requires multiple app security and delivery services including DNS, identity, load balancing, and security-related capabilities. These services might be deployed with the application (in a sidecar to support cloud-native applications) or as a distinct cloud-based service, such as DNS or web app and API protection (WAAP). Both the form-factor—container, virtual machine, and hardware—and the location have an impact on the operational overhead associated with managing these services.

In 2021, while the most likely location for app delivery was at the core, most organizations still distributed both applications and app delivery services across every possible location and operational model.[13]

Thus, the enterprise must contend not only with a growing portfolio of app security and delivery services but also with the increasingly diverse set of operational models that comes with them. Each environment introduces additional complexity and operational debt that negatively impact the organization's ability to adapt. It doesn't matter how adaptable your development organization is if your deployment or operational functions are too rigid to support it or require excessive communication.

---

12 F5, "The State of Application Strategy in 2022."

13 Ibid.

The lack of clarity in the enterprise architecture around app delivery has also led to a skills deficit that continues to grow year over year. App delivery, which is effectively dumped in the technical domain and coupled to infrastructure, requires expertise across multiple functional roles to operate. While the general role of "operations" remains primarily responsible for operating app delivery services, roles in networking, cloud, development, and security are all often assigned responsibility to manage delivery services. This has caused confusion and instability in organizations as team structures abruptly shift to accommodate the cross-functional teams needed to efficiently operate app delivery services.

This results in more time spent communicating than executing. As noted earlier, the impact of communicating is combinatorial with each added member of the group, and thus even more detrimental to adaptability as it further reduces the time available to innovate. A modern approach therefore deliberately seeks to eliminate this confusion and takes advantage of technology to improve the speed of communication, decision, and action. This is generally achieved through abstractions such as the distributed cloud and frameworks like OpenStack that attempt to normalize the diversity of interfaces and control planes and provide a consistent experience across all resources. This has a positive result of increasing adaptability by reducing the number of humans required to operate and scale all relevant components associated with an application or digital service.

Therefore, for businesses to thrive in a digital-as-default economy, automation and event-driven approaches will be required. For app security and delivery, this will also require a shift from traditional operational models to SRE operations, with a focus on observability, tooling, and standardized human processes that enable rapid response to incidents that cannot be resolved by automated systems. SRE operations is the focus of Chapter 7, as its reach and role encompass the entire architecture and is perhaps the most important organizational change needed to modernize IT. Shifting from single-function operational teams to a common, shared operational model will reduce friction and communication penalties across domains.

App Delivery in a Modernized Enterprise Architecture

With application portfolios distributed across multiple locations and models, businesses can no longer rely on "the network" to provide the scale, security, and speed necessary to satisfy user expectations—because there is no "network." Instead, we have multiple networks with varying degrees of influence over security, scale, and performance characteristics.

Based on historical changes in the portfolio, modern applications will continue to consume the app portfolio and overtake traditional applications by 2030, as shown in Figure 3-1. The tight coupling between these applications and container-native environments will unlock the portability that businesses have sought for decades. This will result in greater distribution of applications across disparate environments, which will in turn increase the distributed nature of app delivery services.

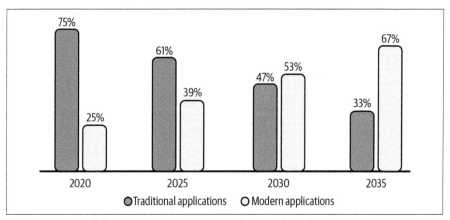

Figure 3-1. Projected change in enterprise app portfolios over time (data from F5's "The State of Application Strategy in 2022")

A new approach is therefore required to serve the needs of applications and a digital business. This approach must enable applications to rapidly respond to changes in performance, availability, or security across one or more infrastructure environments (core, cloud, and edge) with little to no human interaction.

Three key capabilities of a modern app delivery domain stand out as necessary to realize a competitive adaptability ratio:

Automatable

The ability to operate as autonomously as possible becomes an imperative as resources become not only more distributed but also mobile. The ability to easily migrate workloads across environments is rapidly approaching. This will introduce the ability to make deployment and policy decisions based on a variety of factors, including real-time performance and cost. This requires that app delivery services can be harnessed to automation pipelines driven by data to reduce the operators needed to maintain the core and enable greater innovation.

Observable

App delivery services should be natively instrumented to provide the data needed to adjust operating and security policies automatically as traditional methods of monitoring and generating this data add operational overhead that decreases the adaptability ratio. Observability is a key capability to a digital business that must permeate every domain, as the insights needed to drive autonomous capabilities cannot be achieved without sufficiently robust data.

Portable

Workloads will be distributed across the cloud, data center, edge, and end-points. App delivery services should be able to be inserted into the delivery path based on a balance of cost and value to the business as measured by the ability to generate desired business outcomes in any environment, irrespective of the underlying infrastructure. Liberating app delivery from its traditional tether to networking and the technical domain in the enterprise architecture opens new operational models through which the enterprise can accelerate digital delivery and align with desired business outcomes if that architecture incorporates these key capabilities.

Conclusion

Humans have continually modernized methods of communication. From runners in ancient Greece to people riding horses, from the telegraph to the telephone to digital signals, we have continuously taken advantage of technology to optimize delivery. Similarly, an enterprise looking to become a fully digital business must take advantage of technology to optimize app delivery and security.

This requires enterprises to adopt SRE operations and ensure that new architectural elements, such as app delivery and security, find representation in the enterprise architecture so that policies, guidelines, and processes can be associated in a way that enables digital businesses to fully leverage technology. This implies that app delivery should be treated as its own domain, severing its traditional ties with the technical (networking and infrastructure) domain and liberating these functions from being restrained by its policies and processes.

This is integral to the ability of a business to adapt as the location, architecture, and business outcomes for applications and digital services are constantly in flux in a digital world. The choices for this domain will dictate the ability to rapidly adopt new app delivery capabilities to support new technologies such as edge computing, an API-driven economy, and the incorporation of devices as endpoints and sensors across every industry.

The inefficiencies of traditional IT, reflected in Conway's law by the obstacles introduced by increasing numbers of functional silos, will constrain digital transformation initiatives and hamper businesses' efforts to become fully digital unless the trend toward decreasing adaptability is disrupted by modernizing enterprise architecture.

4

Operational Data Is the New Oil

—Mike Corrigan, F5 VP of Engineering,
and James Hendergart, F5 director of Development Operations

Operational data and its potential to produce new business value apply to all types of organizations in all sectors of society and the economy. All domains generate and consume operational data. The ability of organizations to consume enough of the right kinds of operational data, generate valuable insights from that data, and then take correct and timely action determines their ability to achieve and sustain new heights of success in this current age of digital business.

The fact that a saying is a cliché makes it no less true. Many have declared data as the new oil so often that it has become cliché. But it is also a true statement, because operational data, like oil, is an unrefined resource that ultimately enables businesses to extract and create value in the form of derivatives.

Oil is the foundation for more than 6,000 products including "dishwashing liquid, solar panels, food preservatives, eyeglasses, DVDs, children's toys, tires, and heart valves."[1] The value of operational data, like oil, depends largely on refinement and production processes. Indeed, raw data has little value. Rather, it is the information and insights gleaned through careful processing and analysis of the data that produces value.

We already see traditional industries embracing operational data to grow existing business and create new lines of revenue. Those firms that have successfully plotted a path to become a data-driven business are capitalizing on this new strategic capability. For example, the grocery retailer Kroger not only cites

---

1 "Uses for Oil," Canadian Association of Petroleum Producers, accessed May 30, 2022, *https://oreil.ly/D2R54*.

insights as the primary driver of phenomenal growth (14.1% in 2020, aided by a 116% jump in online sales),[2] but it is also entering the insights business by monetizing its data:

> Seeking to leverage its scale and significant insights on customers, the company is seeking to transform its business model with alternative revenue, where it plans to monetize its rich data and make the argument that it can provide CPG [companies] with a superior ROI on ad/marketing dollars (in addition to trade spend) versus traditional channels.[3]

Incumbent architectures, business practices, and skill sets will not deliver value from operational data because they are static and designed for an enterprise architecture that no longer reflects the actual anatomy of their enterprise systems. Static businesses simply cannot adapt and keep up with their customers and competitors. For the CIO, the challenge lies not only in managing and scaling existing business data architectures but also putting in place the technologies, tools, and teams needed to operate an operational data practice at scale.

In this chapter, we explore the pervasive challenge to organizations to become more innovative and think about operational data as a first-class business asset. Operational data, together with corresponding business practices and technology skill sets, enable an organization to govern an operational data platform with discipline and intentionality just like corporate finance, compliance, and risk. This chapter establishes the primary shifts in approach, the architectural ramifications, and the impact on technical skills investment as compared to traditional businesses (i.e., businesses designed to support a static line of business versus those designed to innovate—and how to make progress toward the latter).

Operational Data Platform(s)

An enterprise data practice needs a platform or group of platforms to scale its consumption of operational data (a.k.a. telemetry). This platform should have a flexible architecture for processing data in the right location in the right way, and to provide a consistent framework against which a data governance model can be executed.

---

2 Motley Fool Transcribing, "Kroger (KR) Q3 2020 Earnings Call Transcript," December 3, 2020, *https://oreil.ly/dprcw*.

3 Russell Redman, "Kroger Banks on Burgeoning Sources of Revenue," *Supermarket News*, October 31, 2018, *https://oreil.ly/JDd3Q*.

NEW SOURCES OF DATA

The first step to successfully designing an insights platform is to understand which new types of data are defined as operational data and their sources. All applications, the environments in which they run, and the physical resources used to support them have potential operational data sources.

Applications or application stacks include the app code and everything the app needs to function. Any traditional or modern web application, for example, comprises the app code itself as well as an underlying web server, operating system, and, potentially, hypervisor. The application usually also includes management and orchestration systems. Collect logs and metrics from all these systems to widen the surface area of analytics and correlate otherwise unrelatable data.

Environments point to systems and services unique to a particular cloud or colocation substrate. Container services offered on many public clouds, for example, also offer operational visibility services to go along with them that are designed to report specialized data unique to their environment. Collect this data to determine whether the appropriate remediation should be focused on a given tenant or shifting work to an alternate cloud provider.

Physical resources describe a variety of potential operational data sources that may be overlooked because they are closely tied to physical infrastructure such as space, power, and cooling. We can, for example correlate a power surge on a server that caused a failure in the app and disrupted a set of customer purchases.

The most effective data platforms will strive to achieve full visibility. In fact, a lack of visibility across the entire IT stack results in missing data, which is the number one challenge reported by IT experts in obtaining the insights they need.[4]

At a minimum, operational data can be collected from existing logs, events, and traces used to monitor and troubleshoot the environment. Building on this base, organizations should consider their potential blind spots and work toward gradually illuminating those gaps in pursuit of full visibility through comprehensive data collection.

After achieving a clear understanding of all the potential types of operational data, the next step is creating an inventory of the components that make up a given application/service/digital experience, both internal and external. The

---

4 "The State of Application Strategy in 2022," F5, April 12, 2022, *https://oreil.ly/LHOYj*.

output of this step is a map of the communications mesh among all components. Then through further grouping of components according to any service frameworks that may be used to aggregate telemetry, a reduced and refined view of the best data sources can be created. With this view, combined with the results of the blind-spot research, an organization has built the proper foundation for a data and observability strategy. That strategy should guide the development of a new insights platform and informs plans for enhancing the platform in line with their organization's goals and capabilities.[5]

Note

The composition of the application itself changes as an organization adopts a new digital architecture. The number of microservices and cloud-native runtime components in use can easily number in the thousands for a single workload. This includes many more connections to third-party software-as-a-service (SaaS) services as compared to traditional applications, which are typically designed with many fewer components and very few, if any, third-party SaaS interfaces. Each of these runtime components is a viable operational data source. Identifying the full set of components, their telemetry sources, and which data sets are most valuable is the keen focus of the SRE teams that are the primary actors, as described in Chapter 6.

Other common blind spots in the IT stack are traditional and cloud native/microservices architectures, include the compute layer, nonproxy vantage points, and third-party services. Investigating new telemetry sources across these three areas will provide a starting point from which IT teams can determine which untapped data sources make the most sense to pursue and in what order.

An example of a compute layer blind spot is main server processor trace data. In this case, the data is available but is not being collected. These sources typically provide a voluminous processor execution branch history that needs to be filtered but is nonetheless ready for consumption.[6]

Numerous nonproxy vantage points exist, from the top of the digital stack to the bottom. The term *nonproxy* is meaningful because proxies are usually placed inline with traffic flows, giving them various levels of visibility depending on how they are designed. The proxy vantage point is a natural go-to source for operational data because it already exists to perform other critical functions

---

5 Bradley Barth, "Uncontrolled API 'Sprawl' Creates Unique Visibility and Asset Management Challenges," SC Media, November 5, 2021, *https://oreil.ly/Ks9i1*.

6 Juhi Batra, "Collecting Processor Trace in Intel System Debugger," Intel, accessed May 30, 2022, *https://oreil.ly/vbPJH*.

such as traffic management and security, leaving the nonproxy vantage points as the more likely blind spots. Examples of nonproxy vantage points include the following:

- Packet filters that may be used to implement or optimize a proxy but, in and of themselves, are not proxying network connections and therefore are unique lines of sight.

- The new set of data, control, and management paths described in Chapter 2—DPUs—where infrastructure processing is offloaded from main processors to alternate processing centers. This includes field-programmable gate array (FPGA), GPU, or other auxiliary compute complexes.[7]

- Code instrumented natively in an application or service. The purpose of instrumentation is to track a typical user's path through a business flow as it traverses the various components and services that make up that flow.

Another common blind spot is third-party components. By subscribing to telemetry APIs of third parties, this otherwise invisible source of information increases the accuracy and overall value of insights that can be generated. An ecommerce example is payments processing. Digital payment services are commonly consumed as a third-party SaaS component. In addition to integrating the component itself for completing orders, the companion telemetry service, also exposed by an API, should also be consumed so that this data source can be streamed into the insights platform. Another common type of third-party telemetry source is provided by public cloud services through certain APIs they expose to their tenants.

The proliferation of APIs and their suitability for light yet effective operational data streaming opens the opportunity for standardization in collection architecture. Language-agnostic data formats such as JavaScript Object Notation (JSON) unify the formatting of data to be serialized, and technologies such as Protobuf unify the approach to serializing structured data streamed into time-series data store(s) designed to ingest and hold this information. Interestingly, a new technique addressing the challenge of data ingestion at scale produces multivariate time-series data, a more compact set of data that can be processed 25 times more efficiently than unidimensional streams. Rapid advancements like

---

7 "GPU Trace," NVIDIA Developer, accessed May 30, 2022, *https://oreil.ly/SQAKu*.

this are easily adopted by insights platforms with flexible architectures. They accommodate improvements while simultaneously maintaining certain standards to keep the efficiency and cost equation balanced. This produces increasing value from the platform for the business over time.[8]

Organizations are attracted to free and open source software to build new capabilities for themselves, and the collaboration among users speeds up progress for all participants. In the space of enterprise operational data collection, OpenTelemetry (*https://oreil.ly/UYgRS*), introduced in Chapter 2, is a current example of such a leader. Formed through the merger of two earlier and related projects, this incubating project within the CNCF leads the way. This open community's free and open libraries, APIs, tools, and software development kits (SDKs) simplify and accelerate IT implementation of a common framework for instrumenting and collecting operational data. Once implemented within an enterprise, the APIs used to connect data sources to their destination data stores are standardized, further driving the ability to automate data collection.

The most effective data platforms will employ a flexible architecture for instrumenting systems and collecting operational data. By prioritizing standard formats and APIs yet maintaining liberal acceptance of data collectors and format translators from various vendor-specific formats and serialization techniques, IT teams can work toward increasingly standard formats and APIs over time. This approach is not new. What is new with respect to operational data is that ingestion of such a wide variety of data in various formats requires a decision about how to expose this data to both human SRE teams that need to quickly troubleshoot and remediate suffering systems and to machines that are applying predefined analytics models to generate new insights or remediating issues through automation. So observability for humans and analytics for machines have distinct requirements on operational data that are best determined by SRE and data science professionals, respectively.

New sources of data, such as the application delivery and security services discussed in Chapter 3, require a new operational model for consumption, processing, analysis, and management. IT groups that build a platform to capture all types of data for human and machine processing ready their organizations to proceed to the next phase of transformation: data processing. The correct architecture for processing will take into consideration the location where data is generated, the types of insights that can be drawn from a given data set, the

---

8 Laurent Quérel, "Multivariate Metrics—Benchmark," GitHub, July 23, 2021, *https://oreil.ly/IEBYP*.

availability of processing and storage, and the relative cost of storing, moving, and processing data at various locations. The correct operating model will take into consideration the volume of data, speed of processing, and principles for decision making. We explore both of these and how they relate in the next section.

Having established the blueprint for operational data sources mapped to a given application (a.k.a. workload or set of workloads comprising a digital experience), attention can move on to the key characteristics of a data processing engine for the operational data platform.

DATA PIPELINE AND PRACTICES

As more types of operational data emerge as being critical to the digital enterprise architecture, most enterprises will not be able to build the storage, processing, security, and privacy for all that data at a global scale. Further, technology leaders will find it challenging to expose and use all of that data to the right systems, processes, and individuals within their organization in a compliant fashion. It is for these reasons that a data and insights platform is needed. This is akin to traditional data consolidation efforts and the use of business intelligence platforms for business and customer-focused data. Similar efforts are required today for operational data, to enable analysis to uncover missing insights and produce business value.

How is business value derived from collected data? This is dependent upon the human talent skilled in the various aspects of data management, just as software engineering talent was the key to extracting transactional business value out of the line-of-business systems architected and coded to meet the previous generation of business needs. In fact, code artifacts such as algorithms, mobile device apps, and data models become types of data that fall under the governance and management of the newly formed data team. By treating code as a type of institutional data, an IT team starts to show the signs of driving new business value from a data-first mindset. Those code artifacts can be revised, deployed, and expunged properly as raw materials used to fuel the digital business.

This is similar to the approach taken by DevOps when architecting a development pipeline. Data pipelines, such as the one described in Figure 4-1, require similar processes; thus, many of the practices common to DevOps and SRE operations regarding the use of tooling to deliver business outcomes faster can be applied to DataOps. DataOps is a relatively young practice but, like DevOps and SRE, promises to transform traditional processes into modern, more efficient ways of working.

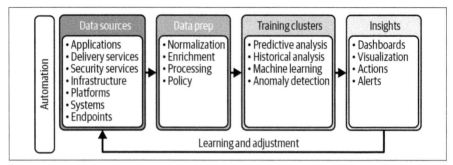

Figure 4-1. A typical data pipeline with automation to enable real-time operations

At the platform layer, an effective architecture accommodates the requirements for data acquisition, protection, management, processing, and exposure.
In contrast to being a relatively static transactional asset (e.g., customer profiles
and history) with engineering resources assigned to maintain a system or systems, data becomes a dynamic raw material that merits its own engineering
resources assigned to curate, search, analyze, and process to solve problems,
discover insights, and enrich over time. This will naturally create a tension as
competition between traditional software engineers and data-focused engineers
with skills across data design, data curation, and data science rises. Investing in
data talent shifts the organization to become more innovative and able to leverage
its data assets.

The Nebulous, Evolving Domain of Data Science

The term *data science* is muddled with controversy. First suggested as
an alternative to *data analysis* in the 1960s, proposed definitions have
traditionally included an emphasis on statistics and numerical analysis.
The professional title *data scientist*, coined in 2008 and attributed to DJ
Patil and Jeff Hammerbacher,[9] today is commonly accepted as a role
with responsibilities focusing on the use of technology to aid in data
analysis, especially machine learning. New roles are emerging that focus
on the operational needs of managing data and insights platforms, but
few standards or job descriptions reflect these roles today.

---

9 Thomas H. Davenport and DJ Patil, "Data Scientist: The Sexiest Job of the 21st Century," *Harvard Business
Review*, October 2012, *https://oreil.ly/LdwKt*.

In terms of the design for the new data and insights platform, a composite architecture takes into consideration the location of data, the types of insights that can be gained from a given data set, the availability of processing and storage, and the relative cost of storing, moving, and processing data at various locations. Unlike traditional customer and business data, which is typically consolidated in a central location, operational data is likely to be more distributed.

For example, some of the data will be processed at the edge by using ML designed for real-time or near real-time decisions based on appropriate AI/ML models. About 35% of organizations expect edge computing to support real-time data processing and analysis, where responses within 20 milliseconds are critical.[10] This is often a requirement in the manufacturing and healthcare industries. A subset of this data will be aggregated for processing and analytics suited for queries that use other types of AI/ML models to discover a different set of insights in line with the needs of that higher aggregation point. Ultimately, the longest-held data will be stored in the most centralized locations specializing in analysis at the highest order of scope. A good example today is ServiceNow (*https://oreil.ly/4iwL9*), which offers a platform for operational information.

Identifying what data needs to be processed where, which data needs to be stored, and what types of analysis to perform on which data sets are all questions that are answered in this area of the new digital enterprise architecture. ML models should be deployed where the insights they produce can be of best use, either locally or centrally. The factors that dictate this are as follows:

- Where can the collected data be stored?
- Where is the data model for processing this data stored locally?
- How long does that data need to be stored before it is processed?
- What type of processing is needed?
- Where is the processing capacity located with respect to the data storage location?

For example, in a video call, the local device is the most likely location for operational data about the quality of the experience to be generated. Given that the right type of processing capability and storage also exists on the device, the ML needed to detect when adjustments to bitrate are necessary to preserve the

---

10 F5, "The State of Application Strategy in 2022."

experience are best run on the device itself. Given an adjustment interval of 10 seconds, even though the flow of operational data is constant, the local device needs to store only 10 seconds' worth of that data at a time while running the local ML, after which it can be expunged. Further, only one reference data set needs to be sent upstream, and that occurs only if an adjustment was needed in any 10-second period; otherwise, nothing is sent.

Once a base design is established by answering the preceding questions at a local device level, the process can be repeated at higher levels of aggregation, producing the appropriate layering of data storage, processing, service adjustments, and operational data forwarding. For a video call originating or terminating on a smartphone, the next level of aggregation might be a single cell tower. At this level, issues affecting the experience of all users connected to that tower become useful, such as failure to initiate a call or unintended disconnects. By applying this reasoning all the way to the centralized computing location (usually a metro or regional data center), needed data is stored in appropriate silos and/or intermingled with appropriate confluences of data from various sources to serve each predefined purpose. Unneeded data is expunged at each point. This layered approach produces targeted insights efficiently because the architecture considers the intended uses of each data set across each layer and at each point in the user experience. The architecture delivers purposed analysis, and treatment of data which, in turn, ensures that the appropriate business value is derived.

Across the architecture and through each layer, the data, the ML models, and the resulting insights are treated as managed objects—like code—with versions, actions, and value being derived continually. They have a lifecycle similar to application code: created according to predetermined requirements, deployed to specific locations, and executed under specified conditions to achieve certain results. Adjustments to the data collected, the way it is analyzed, insights gained, and resulting actions taken perpetuate the data and data model lifecycle driven by business requirements, much like application code iterates in a virtuous cycle of improvement.

Beyond the automated detection and remediation of issues, treating data and data models as code increases an organization's ability to make the most of the insights it discovers. Continuing the video example, the data model used to detect degrading user experience on a local device can be managed like code: kept in a central location, version controlled, updated, and pushed out to devices when appropriate. The next step in the evolution of technology in this case would be to aggregate adjustment data to a central or semi-central location so that a higher-order ML model can be used to detect opportunities to adjust the local ML model (and what to change) so that the update of the local ML model itself is automated. In this way, intelligent use of data, data models, and processing are *adaptable*—a key tenet of the digital enterprise architecture.

While the tension between static and transactional versus adaptable and data-driven digital business certainly manifests in terms of investing in new engineering talent, data engineering should be treated like an expansion of skills and opportunity for growth rather than a detractor. Organizations can and should encourage and invest in data-related skills development of their engineering staff. Engineering efficiencies gained from optimizing maintenance of existing line-of-business applications should be used as leverage to shift learning and assignment of engineering talent to data capture, management, and governance for the organization.

As expertise is gained operating and refining the operational data pipeline, the pattern of finding the right data, developing the algorithms, training the algorithms, and assessing and tuning the outcomes becomes more natural. Further, the catalogs of available models and associated capabilities are increasingly available as a service from third- party providers, giving organizations ever better options for the most common enterprise AI and ML needs. The transformation to data and algorithms over code will accelerate as applications become more dynamic, more microservices based, more dependent on services, and more global in nature. Therefore, the combined approach of building internal experience and leveraging advancements from industry providers and open communities is recommended.

Data Privacy and Sovereignty

As the data about everything is becoming more valuable, society is institutionalizing protecting that data, leading to governance structures that can adjust and tune for the changing needs of society. Governance is evolving to include security, privacy, sovereignty, algorithms, data models, usage, derivative uses, and cascading responsibilities. All of these facets of operational data governance point to an organization's ability to become more adaptable.

The regulatory environment, sovereignty rules, and privacy protections, along with the compliance demands of specialized data, will be an overarching driver of how data is managed, where it is stored, how it's processed, and who/which machines have access to it. New cases are emerging because some machine-generated data formerly in isolation is now being directly shared, aggregated, or otherwise accessed from outside its system. In the next few years, almost all data will be under some kind of compliance regime to help minimize exposure for customers and companies.

One of the biggest challenges of using data today, particularly structured data, is the all-or-nothing approach: someone either is trusted to see all the raw data or has no access to it.[11] One solution that is emerging to deal with this tension is *differential privacy*. It provides a way for access to partial sets of data in such a way that the persons attached to that data are not identifiable. Some start-ups are already using this concept to provide a new level of privacy in critical areas like healthcare and financial services.[12]

Granularity of control over access to data is required to support the governance requirements and mitigate the risk associated with accessing data. This granularity is measured in two dimensions: scope and use. *Scope* is the precision of the data set; more granular means smaller (by field versus row in a table, for example). *Use* is the role of the user, the type of access, and associated conditions. For example, the same user may have multiple roles, triggering the need to access data for different purposes, and each purpose may have associated constraints such as time windows bounding the sanctioned access. The level of granularity required will increase over time, driven by ongoing cases of data exposure abuses and tightening of regulatory constraints in response to them.

Data Governance Evolves

An organization's ability to manage and govern data will be the key to its ability to modernize business with a digital enterprise architecture. This requires a much larger governance approach than has been used previously as human processes incorporated governance into the business processes performed. Governance needs to be built into the digital enterprise architecture and business practices.

Most (80%) organizations say data governance (*https://oreil.ly/mmhll*) is important to enabling business outcomes.[13] Despite this, less than half (43%) either have a data governance program or have implemented a strategy that

11 Adrian Bridgwater, "The 13 Types of Data," *Forbes*, July 15, 2008, *https://oreil.ly/KvwID*.
12 "5 Top Emerging Data Privacy Startups" StartUs Insights, accessed May 30, 2022, *https://oreil.ly/YHqZj*.
13 Heather Devane, "This Is Why Your Data Governance Strategy Is Failing," Immuta, April 8, 2021, *https://oreil.ly/UHfvY*.

is considered immature.[14] Factors that stand in the way of data governance practices are familiar: cost, lack of executive sponsorship, little-to-no business participation, and a lack of prioritization. But the reality is that a digital business depends on operational data. Foot traffic and patterns at physical locations once provided businesses with the insights they needed to make decisions and drive growth. The digital equivalent is operational data. The dependency of a digital business on that data requires viewing data governance as a mission-critical business function, analogous to fiduciary controls governing finance and testing governing code quality.

Data governance requires a framework capable of supporting a data operations practice and enforcing policies that govern access and usage of data while complying with data sovereignty and privacy requirements. Figure 4-2 shows a simple data governance framework that meets these requirements.

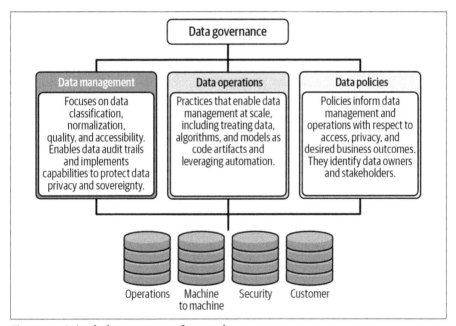

Figure 4-2. A simple data governance framework

---

14 Ataccama, "Data: Nearly 8 in 10 Businesses Struggle with Data Quality, and Excel Is Still a Roadblock," Cision PR Newswire, April 7, 2021, *https://oreil.ly/o35qo*.

Executing on such a framework, even a simple one, will be challenging without employing AI, ML, and automation because of the volume of data ingested, the complexity of the analytics applied, and the speed at which responsive actions need to be taken.

Traditionally, organizations use human interaction as the governance mechanism for data. Digital businesses rely on data to drive decisions for both the business and operations. This means digital governance must be incorporated into the infrastructure and the development cycle so that data management actions are automated. This requires every component across the entire architecture to be capable of executing a governance action. This capability must be designed into every component and applied everywhere, be transparent, self-regulating, and easy for owners to modify. Businesses from more regulated sectors of the economy have a head start because they are already urged via mandates to adopt organizational structures and processes entirely focused on data access and use.[15]

Conclusion

Establishing an enterprise data practice is essential for deriving new business value from insights found in all types of data, as highlighted recently by the emergence of operational data within the increasingly digital enterprise. The journey is typically gradual as real-world constraints of time, budget, and skilled resources slow down the use of available technology, whether from vendors or open source.

The successful building of a data practice depends upon designing an insights platform using an architecture that is based on standards, with flexibility that allows individual pieces to upgrade at a pace in line with any constraints. The three basic elements of the insights platform are data collection, data processing, and data governance.

In parallel, it is paramount for an organization's business practices and technology skill sets to mature in lockstep so that as operational visibility, volume of insights, and quality of insights increase, the business processes and operational procedures also become less static and more dynamic. As the entire organization becomes more familiar with the new mode of operation, IT shifts from a supporter role to a strategic enabler of transformation.

---

15 Immuta and 451 Research, "DataOps Dilemma: Survey Reveals Gap in the Data Supply Chain," Immuta, August 2021, *https://oreil.ly/i4lli*.

5

Moving Beyond
"Fight or Flight"

—Ken Arora, distinguished engineer, F5 Office of the CTO

Most of us have probably seen documentaries set in the African savannah that begin by focusing on a cluster of animals surrounding a key resource, such as a watering hole in the summer heat. This becomes the backdrop for a storyline introduced by the arrival of some visiting predator—wild dogs, a cheetah, perhaps a crocodile—with drama ensuing from there. Each animal at the watering hole is then faced with an instinctive decision: whether to stay and risk a fight, with the ensuing potential for injury, or to instead flee, at the cost of losing access to the precious water and expending energy in the process as well.

At one level, that storyline is an analogue for the cybersecurity position that many modern enterprises find themselves in today: as an enterprise seeks to gain business reward by providing business value to the outside world, it also necessarily exposes itself to risk.

We, however, being human, realize that our responses to threats should not be driven by raw instinct but rather be rooted in a more considered and nuanced decision-making process. We have the ability not only to understand our immediate position but also to postulate future scenarios and evaluate risk versus reward for the range of outcomes. We also have the capacity to plan ahead by taking appropriate proactive steps to reduce the likelihood of negative outcomes, and we can adapt based on the observed results of those plans. Applying this mindset to the realm of security, the risk-reward perspective is an apt one. Specifically, security governance models and decision-making processes must be both value and risk aware, and policies must reflect the risk-reward trade-off.

Embracing a risk-reward approach to security requires a significant shift in the way we think about digital assets. But it is a necessary shift, given the rapid evolution of digital threats and the inability of existing security models to mitigate them.

Helping to make thoughtful, deliberate, and risk-aware decisions with respect to modern application security is what this chapter is all about. The approaches and practices detailed will also provide a general framework for the protection of digital assets, making it useful when designing a modern security architecture.

The Journey Ahead

The first, and foundational, step in this journey is to create an inventory of all the key digital assets of the enterprise. This model must be inclusive of all types of information: structured and unstructured, business and operational. As discussed in Chapter 4, the modern digital enterprise generates a much broader set of operational data than traditional enterprises, and therefore the security-relevant digital asset inventory must encompass all of this digital information.

The second half of this part of the journey is to then mature from a simple enumeration of *what* assets exist, toward understanding *how* those assets are exposed, and to *whom* access to those assets should be granted (and, implicitly therefore, to whom access should be denied). Execution of this strategy is accomplished by enhancing the asset inventory, with a focus on the means used to access those assets and why such access is required. Last, but far from least, the asset inventory must recognize the fact that applications are the primary means by which data assets are accessed; therefore, the inventory must also be able to map from the data assets to the applications that interact with them.

Once an inventory of assets, enriched with the risk-reward profile of each, is created, the complementary half of the work is to apply protections to those assets. This, too, is itself a journey, with different enterprises at different stages of maturity:

- The first level of maturity applies basic security measures across all assets, ensuring that all identified assets have at least a baseline level of protection.

- The next level places specific additional security measures for particularly valuable or risky assets, tailoring the defensive measures to the nature of the asset and the threats against it.

- The final level moves to a more dynamic and adaptive defensive approach, shaping the countermeasures and remediation to the observed real-time behavior.

The implementation of a risk-reward-based security approach can be accomplished through the use of three broad classes of technologies:

Deterministic enforcement tools
These are direct methods of protection, much like a hard shell or armor for an animal. The two most common are authentication and access control. *Authentication* refers to the ability to have a degree of confidence in the attested identity of an actor who wishes to interact with the application, using tools such as passwords, certificates, and behavioral analysis. *Access control* enforces specifically granted rights to an actor, based on the attested identity, such as the right to invoke a specific REST endpoint or to read from a database.

Situational awareness tools
The keen-eyed and far-seeing giraffes of the savannah exemplify this class of capabilities; by detecting and being aware of potential predators early, we can take preventive measures sooner, with higher efficacy, and limit any potential future consequences. Key technologies for these tools are robust operational telemetry tooling and AI-assisted analysis and insight generation, which enable contextualization of the threat, the asset's current posture, and the business value—the raw inputs to a risk-reward-based approach to security.

Risk-aware remediation policies
This class of tools augments purely deterministic defensive methods with adaptive techniques that can dynamically adjust threat response. It accomplishes this by taking into consideration the asset value and impact of compromise. This is the equivalent of a creature that can assess and respond to events on the savannah, much the same way that humans go beyond an instinctual fight-or-flight response.

Because modern applications are the way organizations deliver digital experiences today, the focus of today's operational cybersecurity practices tilts heavily toward the use of these classes of tools to protect applications and APIs, and the workloads and services that support them. The steps in the journey to protect applications are couched as the "crawl, walk, run" progression.

Progressive Sophistication in Application Protection: From Crawling to Running

On the African savannah, a hierarchy of vulnerability exists among the targets of potential predators. The very young, the very old, and the weakest are often the easiest prey. Thus, being able to run faster than others may be enough of a mitigation strategy. In the "crawl" phase of the journey, simply being a harder target than the one next door is viewed as good enough.

Of course, not all targets are equally attractive. If a target asset happens to be particularly interesting for some reason, being faster may not be sufficient. In those cases, an additional level of forethought is appropriate, asking questions such as the following:

- How might this specific predator attack me?
- What defenses do I have?
- What is the impact of failure?

Understanding the nature of the risk and the impact of compromise of an asset represents the "walk" stage of the progression—one that is situationally aware of the threat landscape.

Finally, a particularly intelligent target animal on the savannah might also be capable of contextualizing concerns in light of the current environment. For example, if it is raining, then slipping and falling while fleeing is a real risk. In the digital asset world, this means merging the information from the asset inventory and the asset threat model with the real-time context. An example is not only understanding that the data about an enterprise's financial systems is sensitive and worth protecting, but also recognizing that suspicious requests against that asset are more noteworthy on the day before an earnings announcement than the day after. This is the equivalent of applying contextually driven risk-aware remediation—the "run" stage of our journey.

Figure 5-1 summarizes the stages of the "crawl, walk, run" application protection journey, and the sections that follow dive into best practices within each step of the journey.

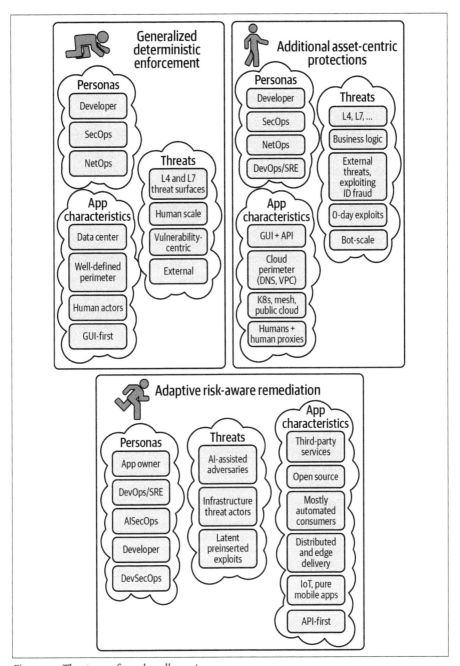

Figure 5-1. The stages of crawl, walk, run[1]

---

1 In the figure, VPC stands for "virtual private cloud" (*https://oreil.ly/zo2We*).

GENERALIZED DETERMINISTIC ENFORCEMENT: THE CRAWLING STAGE

The first step of securing enterprise applications is simply not to be an easy target. If we were protecting a house or an office, this would mean putting locks on doors and alarms on windows. The majority of criminals are opportunistic; therefore, a good deadbolt or alarm system is enough to deter them or easily defeat their attempts.

Protecting enterprise applications in the first stage takes a similar approach, with broad-brush techniques applied consistently across all applications and coupled with basic visibility providing a baseline level of defense. These four techniques are enough to deter opportunistic amateur adversaries, if they have evolved along with the applications they are protecting:

Authentication

In the past, authentication was applied to application consumers who were typically humans seeking access to a monolithic application's GUI, housed within a private data center. As a result, authentication could also reside within that data center. Today, modern applications use a distributed architecture and expose programmatic APIs. Consumers are both human and software, such as automated agents. In addition, applications are increasingly composed of services outside the data center, thus authentication must exist in the world of federated, cross-enterprise, identity stores.

Access control

The first incarnations of access control operated at the network layer; consumers were either "inside" or "outside" a perimeter defined by network IP addresses. Today, consumers are mobile, and applications are distributed; no neat, static perimeter delineates inside versus outside. Access control must be couched in terms of the user identity, as validated by authentication, and classified by groups instead of location.

Conformance checking

Conformance checking of incoming application requests is another critical defensive technique. This defensive measure is required because most systems have significant, often unknown, vulnerabilities that can result in application crashes or even execution of arbitrary malicious code. Attacks such as buffer overflow or SQL injection are examples of this class of vulnerability. Traditional conformance checking focused on layer 7 protocols, typically HTTP. However, as applications are now consumable by nonhuman agents and accessible via APIs, conformance checking at the API layer is now equally important.

DDoS mitigation

One other threat a digital business faces is the potential for an application to become unavailable, either by exhaustion of the resources the application requires or through a catastrophic failure (a.k.a. "crashing the site"). The former—a denial-of-service attack—is often *distributed*, hence the moniker *DDoS*. Like access control, DDoS mitigation has historically been viewed and applied at the network layer with techniques such as rate limiting. But with today's hyperscale public cloud providers, network layer attacks require greater scale, and the application is often decoupled from the network layer. As a result, attackers have moved "up" the stack; modern DDoS attacks such as Slowloris *(https://oreil.ly/fWHZ1)* target the HTTP layer or the logic of the application itself. For example, an attacker might exploit a book-search API provided by a public library by repeatedly asking for a full list of all the books in the library, consuming inappropriate amounts of database resources and internet bandwidth.

Any of these general protections are incomplete without a basic level of situational awareness and audit trail visibility. At a minimum, this means both streaming statistics and alerts. Operations teams need streaming statistics to understand current status and threats, while forensic teams use the statistics to piece together the execution chain of suspected intrusion. Alerts should be triggered for anomalous events, such as an attempted exploit, or by any event that requires auditing for governance. Alerts should be made available either as a log message, directed to a persistent log store, or as a Simple Network Management Protocol (SNMP) trap event. Both streaming statistics and alerts must be consumable by humans via a visualization dashboard, and by a long-term data store.

ADDITIONAL ASSET-CENTRIC PROTECTIONS GUIDED BY SITUATIONAL AWARENESS: THE WALKING STAGE

After having achieved a broad-brush level of protection, the next stage is the asset-centric stage, in which the security strategy is informed by the characteristics of assets being protected. In our home security analogy, after adding locks and alarms, the next logical step would be to identify higher-value assets within the house and apply appropriate additional protection. For example, if there were important paper documents, a theft- and fire-resistant safe might be warranted.

In essence, by taking the time to enumerate and consider appropriate safeguards for higher-value assets—digital assets, in the case of a digital business—based on the unique risks and threats for each, the proper class and strength of mitigation can be applied.

The evolution of digital business brings a greater number of digital assets, along with a variety of asset values and potential threats. Consider the evolution of a straightforward ecommerce site. In a pure task-automation world, that site might merely expose a digital catalog, for which the key threats would be limited to either reduced availability of the catalog or perhaps corruption of the data within the catalog. However, as that same enterprise moves into digital expansion, the catalog might be enhanced to include discounting levels, in order to be automatically ingested by the expanded ecommerce workflow. As a result, a new type of threat—corruption in the discounting data—could yield significant direct monetary loss for the enterprise.

Another dimension of threat surface space emerges when considering attacks that target business availability. Two examples illustrate different threat types, both targeting business availability:

- Sophisticated attackers may attempt to co-opt the application's security logic in their attempt to disrupt application availability. An attacker could mount an attack targeting the authentication logic by creating many failed authentication attempts for legitimate users, consequently locking out those users and making the application unavailable to them.

- Another attacker might target availability by compromising the software supply chain to encrypt critical data resources (a.k.a. *ransomware*).[2] This class of exploits directly targets data necessary to the application and subsequently renders the application unavailable.

The general defensive methods from the "crawling" stage often do not suffice, since they do not fully address new or specialized threats against a richer set of digital assets. However, a more evolved version can be effective, with protection performed in a more specialized manner and strengthened for high-value assets.

---

2 The rise of deliberately injected vulnerabilities into infrastructure software components, commonly referred to as *supply-chain attacks*, is an example of an intentional compromise via third-party components. The SolarWinds breach leveraged exactly such an attack method.

Increasing the strength of authentication via multifactor authentication (MFA) for identified high-value assets will increase the attack effort required. Authentication enforcement can also be hardened. For example, using rate limiting rather than blocking can mitigate the impact of suspicious login attempts and prevent a malicious lockout. Access control can limit which actions authenticated entities can perform.

Security tools for situational awareness also need to evolve; once high-value assets or high-impact threats are identified, a deeper level of visibility should be available for those assets or against those threats. Some relevant examples are as follows:

- Tracking system calls that perform file access, as a means of detecting potential ransomware

- Monitoring the latency and request rates of not just customer-facing APIs, but also key internal APIs as well

- Capturing contextual metadata around authentication attempts, both successful and unsuccessful, to find anomalies and detect potential credential fraud

In summary, this stage is somewhat akin to the progression from the castle-and-moat approach to security, to a defense-in-depth model, where more valuable targets and higher-risk activities are subject to additional layers of scrutiny. This stage brings the concept of asset-value awareness to the security strategy, but still mostly maintains a binary pass/fail view of security without considering the context of each attempted transaction. That next level of sophistication—understanding each transaction's risk-reward profile—is the third stage of the security strategy progression for digital enterprises.

ADAPTIVE RISK-AWARE REMEDIATIONS DRIVEN BY A TRANSACTION-CENTRIC FOCUS: THE RUNNING STAGE

At the core of the next stage of evolution for the digital enterprise is the confluence of two security-relevant concerns and the availability of one game-changing technology:

Concern 1

The threat surface *inside* the application—threats that emanate from the application's workloads and services—is increasing and is today at least coequal with the threat from the exposed, public-facing APIs.

Concern 2

Today's advanced adversaries are much more likely to eventually circumvent any purely deterministic remediations.

Game-changing technology

The use of machine assistance, specifically rule-based systems and ML algorithms, can act as a "force multiplier" by sorting through the massive amounts of data generated by addressing the two aforementioned concerns. This allows a small team of human security operators to scale to meet these new requirements.

The first concern represents a new class of threat vector—compromise of a component or service used by the applications—that has emerged as a primary threat surface. The root cause stems from the evolution of modern application architectures: businesses today rely more heavily on consuming application infrastructure components either from third-party services or as open source software, rather than bespoke software developed in house. In addition, a significant percentage of infrastructure for modern applications is imported from open source projects whose governance falls outside the enterprise's normal models.

This emergence of threats that target the internal application components implies that the security practitioner can no longer exclusively, or even primarily, focus on traditional "outside-in" attacks that target publicly exposed application interfaces. In fact, the most pernicious threats now arise from compromised and vulnerable elements *inside* the application and its infrastructure. A World Economic Forum report on cybersecurity noted that such attacks, sometimes also referred to as *indirect attacks,* have gone from 44% of all attacks in 2020 to 61% in 2021, and that nearly half (44%) of the surveyed CEOs indicated that software supply-chain attacks will have the greatest influence on their organization's approach to cybersecurity in the future.[3]

From the attacker's perspective, a compromise of these core components provides a foothold inside the application itself, which can then be exploited to probe other internal components or install malware—a *lateral-motion* attack mechanism. The security defender now must view each application component with suspicion, adopting a mindset of "assume breach" taken for each component.

---

3 "Global Cybersecurity Outlook 2022," World Economic Forum, January 2022, *https://oreil.ly/7p7lw.*

The second factor—the insufficiency of purely deterministic remediations—is a strategic consequence of the increasingly sophisticated adversaries who also have greater resources available today than ever before, in proportion to the ever-increasing value that can be extracted from compromise of the application. Ironically, just as digital enterprises have embraced AI for improving the application's business value, business adversaries have also embraced AI-assisted attack tools, deployed at very large scale.

Simply considering the reach of modern attackers, the truth of today's internet is that a huge number of internet client devices are compromised, ranging from home internet routers to browsers and mobile apps with Trojan plug-ins. Compounding the issue is that these compromised clients often have access to sensitive authentication collateral on that device. For example, a compromised browser plug-in might have access to the browser's password store, allowing immense sets of usernames and passwords to be harvested, collated, and traded among criminal organizations. *Credential stuffing* attacks can then perform identity fraud by using these compromised username/password lists, at a massive scale, using automated scaling of simple password-cracking tools.

Simultaneously with increased scale, the attacker's use of automation is growing in sophistication; in fact, some attackers have used advanced AI techniques to craft spear-phishing emails and are now using ML techniques to perform intelligent reconnaissance of the target application infrastructure. This AI-assisted recon is combined with more advanced and harder-to-detect attack tactics, whereby determined adversaries couple a *low-and-slow* (low observability profile and long duration) preexploitation phase to a brief, intense exploitation phase, often lasting only seconds or minutes, as data assets are exfiltrated or encrypted.

The resulting impact of the two factors—an increasingly prominent internal threat surface, coupled to more capable, large-scale, AI-assisted adversaries—requires application security practices to evolve in kind:

- Application security must consider not only publicly exposed application interfaces but also the lateral interactions of the workloads and services that compose the application. This can be viewed as the logical evolution from a coarser, asset-granular view to a more modern mindset that is finer grained and component granular, with implementation extensions appropriate for the additional methods and tools used.[4]

- The adversary's use of large-scale, AI-assisted tools implies that the corresponding mitigation strategy should ideally take a two-pronged approach, both (a) analyzing ongoing operational transactions to detect suspicious behaviors associated with long-duration, low-profile activities and (b) simultaneously being capable of rapid response to mitigate the brief, intense exploit phase with subsecond latency, leveraging the prior analysis.

Implementation of this two-pronged approach produces a much larger and richer corpus of data, which theoretically enables the potential for a more in-depth, robust, and ultimately efficacious application security posture. However, achieving this potential requires the processing and analysis of a much higher volume of data—which requires a quantum leap in the ability to process security telemetry. More specifically, the *scale* of data and the *depth* of analysis required for this adaptive approach to application security—in terms of the number of interactions, the volume of correlations to perform, the sophistication of the analysis, and the latency requirements to take effective mitigation—are beyond the capabilities of unaided humans.

The solution is to leverage the game-changing technology of AI assistance, which provides the required quantum leap in the volume and speed needed for the risk-reward data analysis of each transaction. Just as the next step in the evolution of the digital enterprise is the AI-assisted business, in which automated, data-driven systems are used to improve the efficiency of digital experiences, the protection of these next-generation applications must leverage automation and ML algorithms.

Once a security strategy adopts a mindset that operates at a transactional level, security controls must be applied at the granularity of internal components. Therefore, visibility must exist, and the system must be capable of applying remediating actions to internally initiated transactions—implying that identity and authorization solutions must be enhanced. Authentication and access control tools must now embrace the notion of identity for application components.

---

4 This couching of the problem statement may also sound familiar to readers exposed to the zero trust security model, which also focuses on identity (the *who*) and least privilege (the *what*); in that sense, this approach can be viewed as the evolution of the zero trust mindset, applied to every system interaction.

Visibility must also evolve in order to detect the low-profile preexploit activities occurring internal to the application.

In addition, implicit in this mindset is the notion that visibility and assessment are ongoing and continuous. In the adaptive, risk-reward-aware stage of the application security journey, authentication and access control implementations must embrace this mindset by treating confidence scores and access rights not as session-granular, periodically evaluated checks, but as checks that occur for every transaction.

Specifically, tools must evolve in the following ways:

- The security strategy must extend the reach of authentication and access control from merely being at the perimeter of the application to being able to monitor the behaviors of the component workloads and services that compose the application.

- *Visibility* must be enhanced to report on actions not only for APIs at the application perimeter but also actions within the application, including both "east-west" traffic flows, and any system calls invoked by application components.

- *Augmentation* of the deterministic protections of the system is required to perform adaptive subsecond remediation of transactions that fall above a policy-driven risk-versus-reward threshold, often being the response to the intense exploitation phase of a previously undetected compromise. This implementation of subsecond response requires continuous assessment from AI-assisted analysis fed by the deeper visibility mentioned previously.

Embracing AI assistance enables much higher *scale* threat analysis, as the scale requirement emerges from the need to monitor threat surfaces "inside" the application. However, a related observation is around the *depth* of analysis required: to detect the potential compromise of the deterministic protections applied to any one of the large set of application components, the system must perform a deeper analysis of observed intercomponent interactions. With this approach, the actual per transaction risk/reward metric can be contextualized with a more dynamic, continuously updated assessment of risk based on real-time behavior observation, and reward based on business value.

Today's advanced threats will be tomorrow's norm, with those threats being powered by potent and persistent adversaries who will find means to circumvent the deterministic security controls that were the bread-and-butter of yesterday. This will force application security technologies to embrace a transaction-granular, more adaptive view of application security—one that is risk-reward aware and leverages machine assistance to achieve the scale and speed needed. Couched in technology terms, the AI-assisted business requires an AI-assisted security solution.

From Concept to Practice: How the Rubber Hits the Road

The outside-in perspective of the previous section is useful to provide context for the technology leader who must define an application protection strategy for a digital business. This is no simple task. Despite the lack of inclusion of security as a core discipline in traditional enterprise architecture, its practices and policies have nonetheless become a staple addition to IT and the business alike. But the almost ad hoc adoption of security practices, tools, and technology has been a mostly defensive response, with solutions often hastily put into place as a reaction to an existing or imminent threat.

Security as an enabler of digital business has yet to make its way into the collective IT and business conscience; its focus is largely on data. In a digital business, security must expand to include the applications and interfaces through which attackers and users alike interact with data.

This section highlights some of the highest-value practices that will enable technology leaders to develop a modern governance framework for building security into an enterprise architecture for digital business. The practices are presented in the form of a maturity progression, decomposed along the following three dimensions:

- Understanding of protection needs: asset inventory and risk awareness

- Robustness of policy: authentication and access control

- Awareness and responding: from visibility to actionable analysis to automated remediation

IS IT AN ASSET OR LIABILITY (OR BOTH)?

The modern enterprise has assets, both physical and virtual. Governance of physical assets (including real estate, equipment, and inventory) has a long history and well-established procedures, codified into a variety of business processes such as accounting, insurance, and loss prevention. In contrast, the governance of virtual assets is newer and less well structured.

Ironically, however, for most of today's digital enterprises, the value of a company's virtual assets, especially its digital assets (including customer data, intellectual property, and the general digital exhaust of automated workflows) exceeds the value of its physical assets. In 2020, intangibles, which include intellectual property and digital assets, "evolved from a supporting asset into a major consideration for investors—today, they make up 84% of all enterprise value on the S&P 500, a massive increase from just 17% in 1975."[5]

The relevance of asset governance maturity is clear when considering that without an inventory, it is impossible to assign higher-valued assets additional security, since there is no formal enumeration of the assets. Once an asset inventory has been created and enhanced to characterize the nature of the exposure, additional layers of threat-specific protections can be provided for that asset. Then key assets can be mapped to the *who* and *whom* attributes of the transaction. This also requires the inventory be granular down to the level of application workload components, treating workloads as first-class digital assets.

The high-level asset-understanding maturity model can be seen in Figure 5-2.

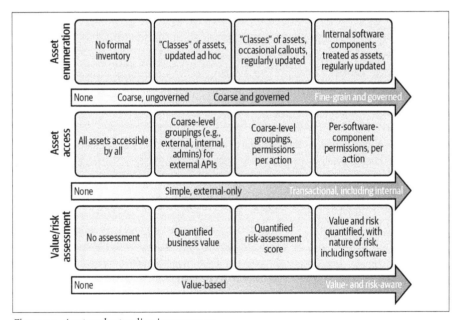

Figure 5-2. Asset understanding journey map

Each of these dimensions has several questions to consider:

---

5 "Financial Impact of Intellectual Property and Cyber Assets Report," Aon, 2020, *https://oreil.ly/jw1lo*.

How are assets enumerated?

A mature asset understanding will include an ongoing governance model and distinguish between classes of assets, such as customer data versus payment data. It will also integrate with the development pipeline, so that software components are treated as assets.

Are asset actions and access specified?

A mature asset understanding will not only include who is permitted to take action upon an asset but also distinguish between actions, such as specifying read versus write access.

Does the inventory quantify value and risk?

The value of an asset to the business, along with the nature and cost of its risks such as compliance, licensing, and brand implications should be included in the asset inventory.

PUT IT IN WRITING: AUTHENTICATION AND ACCESS CONTROL AS POLICY BUILDING BLOCKS

An inventory of assets provides a great foundation for securing the digital enterprise. However, that information must be translated into enforceable actions to realize actual security benefits. The *security policy* is the embodiment of enforcement actions—what actions to take, and when to take them.

Note

Care must be taken not to excessively inhibit the accessibility of data and systems with an overly strict or rigid security policy. Inaccessibility of systems today is a major challenge for organizations, with "less than 34% of employees [saying] that data created within their department is widely available on their enterprise systems."[6] Introducing further friction through security into the process of sharing data more broadly across the organization can impede progress toward becoming a digital business. Security policies and controls that degrade performance, in particular, are prone to being disabled, defeating the purpose of implementing them in the first place. More than three-quarters (76%) of organizations admitted they would disable security for as little as a 1% improvement in performance.[7] It is important, then, to view security policies from the perspective of protecting digital assets in conjunction with their ability to remove friction from processes that, because of digitization, increasingly span departments and data silos.

---

6 Steve Dertien and Will Hastings, "The State of Digital Thread," PTC, July 2021, *https://oreil.ly/evOMC*.

7 "The State of Application Strategy in 2022," F5, April 12, 2022, *https://oreil.ly/dlwLV*.

In practice, a security policy spans multiple layers—network, protocol, and application—and functional areas. However, two of the most relevant areas are authentication and access control.

Figures 5-3 and 5-4 present journey maps for authentication and access control, with a set of specific considerations as enterprises progress through the three stages of application security maturity.

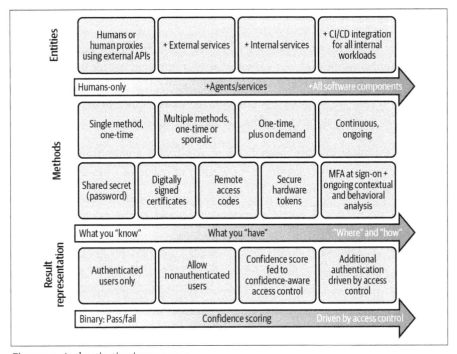

Figure 5-3. Authentication journey map

Some of the specific questions when evaluating authentication solutions are as follows:

How robust is the space of entities that can be authenticated?
A fully robust solution, in addition to human and software consumers, must be able to authenticate even the software components that are used to construct the application. This capability defends against the most pernicious attacks, in which internal components have been compromised.

How rich is the set of methods used to authenticate an entity?
Passwords are easily harvested, and large databases of compromised credentials exist. Certificates are revocable but often have a long shelf life. Because advanced adversaries can defeat such schemes, either by compromise or by hijacking a preauthenticated session, the next generation of authentication methods must be able to perform continuous assessment and consider contextual data such as user behavior patterns.

How is the authentication decision represented?
More sophisticated systems go beyond a simple binary yes/no and can present a more nuanced response with a score reflecting the confidence that the entity is the attested one. Additionally, this score should be updated in real time based on observed behaviors and allow for additional authentication steps to be taken to increase confidence.

Access control logically goes hand in hand with authentication, as a key input to an access control system is the identity of the actor—the *who*. Figure 5-4 is a summary maturity model.

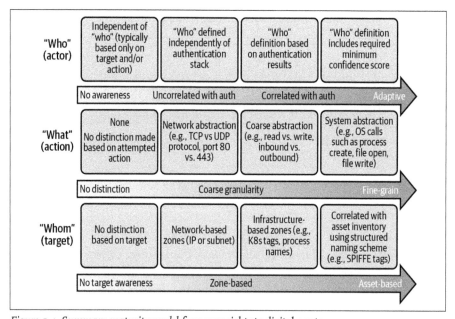

Figure 5-4. Summary maturity model for access rights to digital assets

Some of the most important considerations in this space are as follows:

What is the definition of actor?
The authentication and access control solutions should agree on the definition of the actor and operate at the same layer. The access control system should have the ability to consume a confidence-based authentication "score" and be able to provide feedback to the authentication system to request additional authentication. For example, if the access control system requires a high score to permit a high-value transaction, it may be appropriate for access control to request two-factor authentication (2FA) if the current score does not meet the threshold.

What abstraction is used to specify the allowed rights for an actor?
Traditional firewalls can permit or deny access but are allowed to use only network abstractions, such as network protocols, IP fields, and perhaps HTTP methods. Other solutions make distinctions at a slightly higher level, perhaps read versus write access for files, or create versus kill for process control. However, given the breadth of attack surfaces, it is best to have finer-grain control of actions, and the interception of system calls is often the most useful. For example, ransomware encryption attacks can be detected by noting not only the use of file read and write activity but also calls to encryption routines and random number generators.

Finally, how does the access control system describe the destinations, or targets, of the actions the entity is attempting?
Again, network firewalls use network abstractions or zones such as "inside," "outside," and "DMZ." This abstraction is often less relevant with virtualized and overlay networks coupled to dynamic workloads. Other solutions are tied to specific infrastructures, such as tags specific to a Kubernetes instance or to a specific cloud provider. A more robust approach is to be platform independent and use the asset vocabulary developed for the asset inventory model.

WHAT DID I JUST SEE, AND SHOULD SOMEBODY DO SOMETHING ABOUT IT?

While it would be nice if protection mechanisms such as authentication and access control were ideally implemented and sufficient to stop all attackers, that does not reflect today's reality. Whether by oversight, imperfect gatekeeping techniques, insider compromise, or pure luck, some attacks will get past the predefined policy control mechanisms. In short, we must embrace the zero trust axiom of "assume breach."

Recent advances in AI technologies, most notably statistical analysis, deep neural networks, and decision trees, have the ability to change the game. Some of today's advanced application protection solutions can detect anomalous behaviors with subsecond latency, quickly enough to greatly reduce, if not entirely eliminate, the impact of a compromise. The term *AISecOps* has been coined for the discipline that marries operational cybersecurity with AI to stop security breaches in their tracks.

If anomaly detection is the engine of AISecOps, data is the oil that keeps the engine running, as described in Chapter 4. And the drivetrain that allows the engine to accomplish the goal—breach containment for AISecOps—is automated remediation. The capacity for automated remediation for a wide variety of conditions in a digital business is a recurring thread woven into the design of a modern enterprise architecture. This capability is mirrored in other domains, such as noted in Chapter 3 within app delivery as a means to mitigate threats to performance and availability.

Figure 5-5 enumerates the key dimensions of AISecOps and the maturity progression along each dimension.

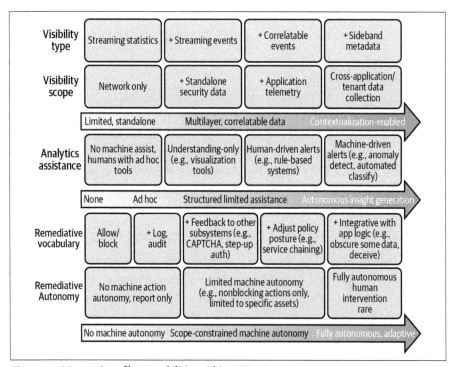

Figure 5-5. Maturation of key capabilities within AISecOps

The following are some specific self-assessment questions related to an organization's AISecOps maturity:

What sort of data is available for AISecOps to analyze?
Can the system ingest data from all layers: network, protocol, API, and application? Can it ingest both statistics and events? A robust system should accept both and be able to correlate across statistics and events, simply using time as the correlation index. Additionally, can the system ingest sideband data that can be used to contextualize the event, such as understanding if a client device is a member of a botnet, or looking across applications to see if a coordinated adversary campaign is in progress?

How deeply is machine assistance integrated into analysis workflows?
Traditional forensic analysis made very limited use of compute resources, sometimes using machines just to filter based on keywords or time windows. More modern stacks provide advanced visualization capabilities for efficient data exploration, and some systems allow user-defined rules that can trigger and alert in real time.

How rich is the space of remediating actions available, and which can be automated?
A basic firewall can allow or block a transaction. However, this approach leaves little room to accommodate the gray areas that enterprises often face. A bank may rightfully be concerned about fraudulent money transfers, but at the same time, not want to lose business. "Softer" actions, such as using a CAPTCHA or requesting MFA, is preferable to outright blocking even if it introduces friction. These can be integrated into the business logic, where the action might depend on a transaction's monetary value.

How long until action can be taken?
Because containing the scope of damage is highly correlated with the time until action is taken, the more autonomy granted to the system to remediate, the lower the time to remediate and the greater the likelihood that damages will be small or nonexistent. To address the most common concerns around granting full autonomy—false positives and explainability—the system's suggested response can be monitored, with adjustments as needed, until an acceptable false-positive rate is achieved. Explainability is best addressed by judicious choice of AI algorithms: the results of algorithms like decision trees or anomaly detectors are often more easily understood by humans than other techniques like deep neural networks.

Conclusion

Historically, enterprises viewed security as a sort of tax on business, often an afterthought consideration to be addressed once the "real work" of developing the application was completed. However, as today's enterprises transition into the digital expansion phase of digital transformation, with increased focus on modernizing the enterprise architecture, it becomes more evident that a business's key assets are its digital ones. Therefore, a more proactive and considered approach to application security is not only required but also must be integrated into the application development lifecycle.

Start with basic protections so that the enterprise's assets are not viewed as being low-hanging fruit for attackers. Just as basic physical security practices place alarms and cameras at the most convenient ingress points, such as doors and windows, basic application security should at least have basic safeguards at its public-facing interfaces.

Of course, not all digital assets are equal; some will be more valuable or risk greater damage if compromised. Thus, the strength of the defense must be proportional to the value of the asset, implying that the enterprise must know its assets and values. Consequently, the next stage in the security journey is understanding the assets that exist, their value and risk profile, and, ideally, who needs access. Executing on that information involves placing additional protections, tailored to the nature of the threats, for those key assets.

In the final stage of the journey, the enterprise accepts that there is no silver bullet, no foolproof scheme that deterministically catches all adversaries. Instead, any digital experience both presents a business reward and exposes the business to risk. Therefore, the sober perspective understands that breaches to the deterministic policies will occur and adopts a risk-based, AI-enhanced backstop mechanism to catch any escapes.

Both applications and the threats against them are constantly evolving; thus ongoing security governance is vital. From an engineering perspective, baking security into the application development process as a first-class concern is the best way to succeed. However, engineering practices cannot fix an organization's views on cybersecurity nor the reporting structure of its CISO. From an organizational perspective, the recognition and elevation of the role of CISO—and by extension, security—can signal a significant shift in an organization's prioritization of security that results in greater acceptance of responsibility for security across every domain and role.

| 6

Observability and Automation

—Michael Wiley, F5 VP of Engineering and CTO of Applications

Isaac Asimov is most notably associated with the ethics and morality of robotics, thanks to his series of short stories that eventually became the well-known novel, *I, Robot*. As with most science fiction focused on AI, the theme of digital processing being superior to that of human capabilities rises to the surface.

Traditional enterprise architectures were designed to support human operators and decision makers. Team structures, systems, and even applications were all designed on the presumption that human beings, following manual processes, would be at the helm.

Digital service means the service can self-detect its customer experiences, bottlenecks or deviations in the workflows, or new distribution of customer demands. As such, the digital service should have built-in "sensors" to detect these signals and ways to quickly bring changes to the digital service.

In a digital business, the volume of information generated and requiring immediate processing and analysis would overwhelm even an army of human operators. To return to the principle that "form follows function," today's enterprise architectures constrain business to the limits of human scale. A digital business requires the capability for *digital* scale: the capability to automatically detect bottlenecks or performance deviations in the customer experience. To achieve this, digital services should have built-in sensors. Furthermore, a system must exist to analyze the signals produced by the sensors and detect any problems as well as a means to quickly mitigate them. In other words, a traditional enterprise architecture forces business function to follow its form, that of human scale. To reverse this and enable digital scale, the enterprise architecture must be expanded to include observability and automation as core capabilities.

87

The Value of Observability and Automation to a Digital Business

Observability is a relatively new term. It describes the capability of an organization to infer the internal state of systems, digital services, and ultimately, the business itself from a set of outputs. The presence of a toy car on the floor of your living room might lead you to infer that a young child is somewhere in the house. Similarly, the state of multiple systems might lead you to infer that a performance problem exists with the application processing orders that negatively impacts the business.

It is helpful to view the digital business as a system similar to a living organism that is constantly threatened, changing, learning, and adapting. Such a system *must be observed* to infer state. The state of a human being might be inferred by observing behavior and taking measurements such as white blood cell counts and temperature. These are technically outputs of the state of your health, as both will rise above established norms if you have an infection. When you measure outputs, you can achieve a reasonable inference of the system and communicate the potential responses needed within the system.

This means that observability is not a replacement for the monitoring of a system. In truth, monitoring is a critical activity that allows an organization to gain observability into the health of the digital business. *Monitoring* is the process of measuring outputs, and those outputs are fed into a more intelligent system capable of inferring the state of the overall system from those measures. As with a doctor, the more measures (outputs) that can be gathered, the better the diagnosis—the inferred state of the system.

For a long time, the ability to measure outputs did not matter so much, because high-cardinality dimensions were rarely needed. With a typical monolithic system, you had a single application tier, limited infrastructure, minimal systems, and one database. This is no longer the case. Refactoring a monolithic application to many microservices, cloud endpoints, virtualization of systems, APIs, and expanded network infrastructure creates a new paradigm that requires observability.

As shown in Figure 6-1, the value proposition of observability aligns with larger business goals and operational objectives:

Bettering the customer experience

Did that recent change or addition of a feature within the application impact the overall customer experience? Knowing your application and customers' experience is critical. Having the data (telemetry) that describes the customer impact of changes occurring within the overall system will provide enterprises with the means to make decisions on technology placement, investments, and the impact of application advances.

Cost awareness and impact

A robust observability strategy will provide businesses with the data to articulate the actual cost per "unit" measurements (e.g., cost per user acquisition, price per unit of compute, storage, bandwidth, etc.) needed to scale and/or right-size overall technology investments. Through the collection of many instrumented applications and systems, this metric thinking will drive further IT efficiencies into the cost per transaction, which is a measure of the cost to align execution (scale and deployment location decisions) with business outcomes (margins on digital sales).

Faster time to market / velocity

Observability can also offer technology leaders an understanding of their software delivery pipeline and uncover automation opportunities. Leaders can gain an understanding of the software delivery pipeline by measuring the velocity of software and infrastructure releases across multiple teams. This can then describe the capabilities of the enterprise delivery system. Uncovering automation opportunities offers the ability to reduce the time to market, effectively improving the organization's ability to adapt and deliver new capabilities to customers.

Higher quality of code releases

Measuring the quality of code releases by using quantitative measures such as cyclomatic complexity, weighted micro function points, and Halstead complexity measures and their impact on the operational teams is often missed in the observability space. Instrumenting for these measures is advantageous for achieving operational efficiencies and addressing code-quality issues. The cost of poor-quality code reached an estimated $2.84

trillion in 2018 in the US alone, 37.46% from operational failures.[1] Releasing software (products) that cause an impact to the operation is not an acceptable practice.

Optimizing where it makes sense
As a technology leader, you have many optimization targets that need to be very data driven within these initiatives. Observability allows you to immediately infer correctly what impact automation will have upon the operations, deployment, and development teams.

Application reliability
It is well understood that application reliability is a necessary measurement in the overall application, infrastructure, and system design. This is often articulated in terms of the number of 9s of availability, stated as a percentage of uptime, e.g., 99.999%. However, this is often implemented incorrectly, proxying response time as measured by a ping or an HTTP request. This type of metric does not accurately describe the full system availability. A better set of metrics for application reliability is explored in depth in Chapter 7.

Risk management
Unfortunately, many products, applications, and infrastructure services are not well enough instrumented nor verbose enough to accurately identify risk opportunities. You do not have to look too far in the past to recognize this challenge, as the scrambling to address Log4j vulnerabilities demonstrated. Distributed workloads make this extremely challenging as well. Building an observability strategy that incorporates measurements on what vendor products, applications, systems, infrastructure, tooling, and services are performing in their intended state and runtime is needed to ensure that risk management is addressed properly.

Both business and operational benefits rest on two key capabilities that do not exist in a traditional enterprise architecture: observability and automation. The rest of this chapter is dedicated to these two capabilities, both of which are critical domains within a digital enterprise architecture. But first we need to explore the measures needed to inform observability.

---

1 Herb Krasner, "The Cost of Poor Quality Software in the US: A 2018 Report," Consortium for IT Software Quality, September 26, 2018, *https://oreil.ly/3tlhH.*

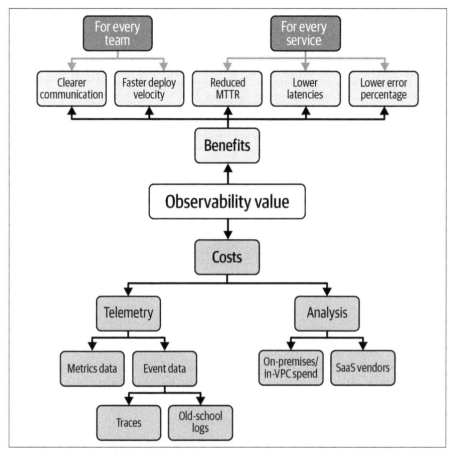

Figure 6-1. The value of observability in the enterprise is found in business and operational benefits and reduced costs[2]

The Measures That Matter

Before diving into observability, let's unpack telemetry a bit as this term tends to be used to describe data needs from collection to management to analytics. What we are really attempting to articulate with the term *telemetry* is the metrics, logs, and tracing data needed to achieve our end-state goals.

Each is a distinct type of telemetry, the use of which overlaps with the others, as shown in Figure 6-2, to produce an observable system. This might be old hat for many, but it is worth revisiting a bit of the definition and intent of each.

---

2 In the figure, VPC stands for "virtual private cloud" (*https://oreil.ly/zo2We*).

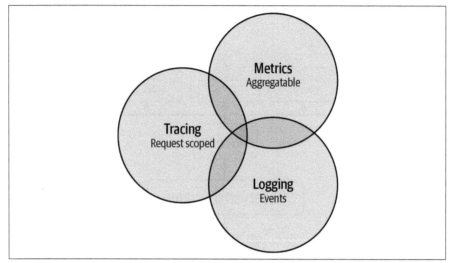

Figure 6-2. The three distinct types of telemetry combine to produce observable systems

METRICS

Metrics are a set of time-series data, a type of data with an x-axis measurement such as time or another variable, and a y-axis measurement such as the value of a variable or an event. Examples of time-series data are public transport utilization, oil prices, population growth rates, and tax revenue. Data is collected over time by an organization with the goal of understanding how things change over time. There are many ways to analyze this type of data.

You can think of time-series data as a key-value pair (set), as shown in Figure 6-3. You may have heard of the term *key-value* before, but in time-series data, it is important to know what that means. To simplify things: the *value* is a property or measurement, and the *key* is its timestamp.

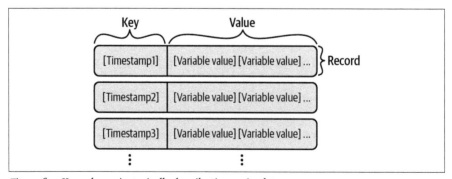

Figure 6-3. Key-value pairs typically describe time-series data

LOGGING (LOGS)

Every company these days is engaged in *logging*, from systems, infrastructures, and applications. These records are used to enable developers to debug their code, provide insights into the health of the system, and even help with regulatory compliance. Logs typically are divided into three types: application logs; server, or system, logs such as the one shown in Example 6-1; and infrastructure logs. The explosive growth of cyberattacks and reliance on the internet have led to a fourth type of log: security events.

Example 6-1. A typical web server log

```
{"timestamp": "2022-07-06T17:53:12+00:00", "host": "example.com",
 "uri": "/setCurrency", "upstreamStatus": "502",
 "upstreamAddr": "10.12.0.13:8080", "requestMethod": "POST",
 "requestUrl": "example.com/setCurrency", "status": 502,
 "userAgent": "python-requests/2.21.0", "latency": "0.000",
 "protocol":"HTTP/1.1", "requestTime": "0.000", "upstreamConnectTime": "-"}

{"timestamp": "2022-07-06T17:53:11+00:00", "host": "example.com",
 "uri": "/cart", "upstreamStatus": "200",
 "upstreamAddr": "10.12.0.13:8080", "requestMethod": "GET",
 "requestUrl": "example.com/cart", "status": 200,
 "userAgent": "python-requests/2.21.0", "latency": "0.063",
 "protocol":"HTTP/1.1", "requestTime": "0.063", "upstreamConnectTime": "0.000"}

{"timestamp": "2022-07-06T17:53:10+00:00", "host": "example.com",
 "uri": "/product/LS4PSXUNUM", "upstreamStatus": "200",
 "upstreamAddr": "10.20.0.11:8080", "requestMethod": "GET",
 "requestUrl": "example.com/product/LS4PSXUNUM", "status": 200,
 "userAgent": "python-requests/2.21.0", "latency": "0.030",
 "protocol":"HTTP/1.1", "requestTime": "0.030", "upstreamConnectTime": "0.000"}
```

TRACES

What are application traces and distributed tracing? An application *trace* is a sequence of events that happen to an application. *Application traces* are used to better understand the way an application performs in various scenarios or environments and can also help identify performance bottlenecks. The data generated by the trace can be analyzed using many tools.

Distributed tracing uses the construct of span and session IDs. *Span IDs* are used to mark data packets with a timestamp, so that data can be correlated regardless of where it is coming from or going to. These span IDs represent the endpoints of the trace, and each packet will have its own unique ID that corresponds to the session ID. You can think of distributed tracing as a *per hop* performance measurement, as a request or action is performed across many infrastructure components. The combination can then be used to generate visualizations that show the path of packets through systems, services, infrastructure, and applications, as shown in Figure 6-4.

Distributed tracing allows business and application stakeholders to visualize relationships and determine performance across an application path, taking something that is nonrelational with different data sets/types and inferring something like latency across a system (application calls).

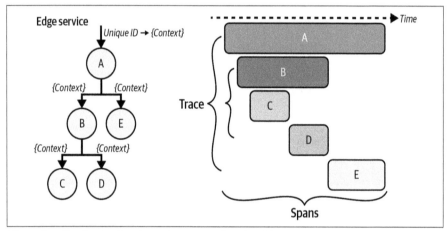

Figure 6-4. Simple visualization using span and session IDs

You might think of this as an application and system performance measurement like *traceroute* for application calls across multiple systems. It provides a per hop behavioral view of your application.

The support for distributed tracing and the propagation of the data it generates is not standard today despite broad industry momentum toward the adoption of OpenTelemetry. Technology leaders should consider this support a fundamental requirement as they modernize enterprise architecture.

The Need for Instrumentation

Organizations that audit their sources of telemetry to ensure they have access to the measures that matter will find an abundance of some (such as logs) and a dearth of others (such as distributed tracing data). A complete audit that covers systems and services across the core, cloud, and edge is almost certain to find gaps in coverage.

The biggest obstacle to achieving observability today is missing data.[3] This is problematic because, as discussed in Chapter 4, data (telemetry) is a critical component for digital business. Over 30% of true data-driven businesses today experience growth despite macroeconomic challenges.[4] Decisions based on telemetry will be made in both a human and programmatic context that impact business processes, financial decisions, software application investments, customer experience, and product delivery. Organizations that struggle to achieve observability will find it difficult to survive, let alone compete, in a data-driven digital economy.

Without the instrumentation of the underlying applications, infrastructure, and processes that make up modern digital services, problems with a single component can quickly cause failures elsewhere in the system that negatively impact a customer's experience. Without instrumentation—and a means to collect the measures it produces—technology leaders are left with data silos that obscure the true value of data. These silos remain the single largest obstacle, preventing 89% of businesses from progressing on their digital transformation journey.[5]

Unfortunately, for decades, the ability to collect measures (telemetry) from systems and applications has been left to ad hoc, team-specific solutions. Agent-based options and add-in components have been the norm since the adoption of the internet and have propagated the problems associated with opinionated collection of telemetry. Neither the traditional enterprise architecture nor applications built atop it have been infused with the ability to generate telemetry natively. The result is disconnected data silos across IT that cause confusion and lead to delays in discovering the cause of outages and performance problems. Both businesses and IT shoulder the cost of missing telemetry, which can leave them:

- 10 times less likely to be able to perform historical performance comparisons
- 9 times more likely to miss conditions indicative of an attack
- 10 times more likely to miss the root cause of performance degradation[6]

---

3 "The State of Application Strategy in 2022," F5, April 12, 2022, *https://oreil.ly/5oK4K*.

4 Laurence van der Sande et al., "Why You Need to Capitalize on the Rise of the Data-Driven Enterprise," Accenture Insights, May 21, 2021, *https://oreil.ly/Q6ua5*.

5 "2022 Connectivity Benchmark Report," MuleSoft, *https://oreil.ly/fdMmL*.

6 F5, "The State of Application Strategy in 2022."

Given the importance of each system and process that makes up a modern enterprise application, it is paramount that they are observable; that is, they must be instrumented.

OBSTACLES TO INSTRUMENTATION

Achieving the needed level of instrumentation requires significant investment because of the complexity of modern internet-scale applications and the broad adoption of APIs as a primary method of integration for business, applications, and operations. Technology leaders embrace APIs for their value in reducing the cost to maintain their core; the use of APIs produces an average 63% reduction in costs that shifts the balance of resources toward innovation.[7] Other organizations adopt APIs as a modernization method.

Nearly one in three (30%) technology leaders modernize applications by refactoring.[8] Refactoring often results in moving applications from a monolithic construct to a microservices architecture, in which functions within the application are broken up, built, and deployed as discrete containerized or atomic services, as shown in Figure 6-5. The telemetry and operational challenges become progressively more complex with this approach, as the number of components increases exponentially.

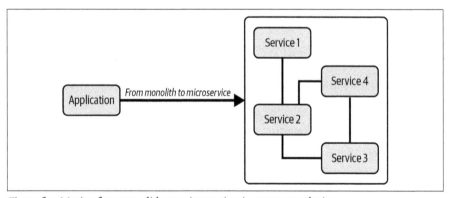

Figure 6-5. Moving from monoliths to microservices increases complexity

It is no longer acceptable to *not* treat telemetry as a first-class citizen in software—and hardware—products and services design. If data determines the health and well-being of a digital business, the generation of telemetry must

---

7 "4 Steps to Create a Data-Driven Business," 2020, MuleSoft, *https://oreil.ly/hx14r.*
8 F5, "The State of Application Strategy in 2022."

be a priority. Businesses need a level of telemetry that is verbose, complete, documented, nonopinionated, delivered in near real time, and vendor neutral, as described in Chapter 4.

The growth of applications and systems, along with the distributed nature of both, is increasing at exponential rates. Nearly every business (97%) plans to take a best-of-breed approach to the distribution of workloads across at least two different core, cloud, and edge locations as a strategy to comply with regulations and boost resilience of digital services.[9] This creates an extensive telemetry demand. If the application, service, or system is opaque, or the impact of a particular infrastructure, system, application, or service is not visible through a telemetry pipeline, the enterprise will be compromised, operationally limited, and at a larger business disadvantage. Enterprises might abandon a product or service, as this state increases the cost to maintain and the potential to do harm. A nontrivial 33% of consumers will walk away from a business they love after just one bad digital experience.[10] Missing telemetry is the single biggest challenge standing in the way of businesses' ability to prevent bad digital experiences due to outages or performance degradations.[11]

SURMOUNTING INSTRUMENTATION CHALLENGES

Much like Java Spring Boot, which natively comes with the metrics library Micro-meter, auto-instrumentation of applications is paramount. Choosing application libraries built in a vendor-neutral way eliminates reliance on the developer to decide which instrumentation to include apart from custom metrics that may be required. Auto-instrumentation also enables technology leaders to define standards for generation that dramatically reduce the time and cost associated with normalizing telemetry for processing and analysis. Enterprise Management Associates analyst Torsten Volk adds the following:

> *Auto-instrumentation addresses the significant risk of developers not fully instrumenting their code, and therefore, creating monitoring blind spots that can bring significant operational risk.*[12]

---

9 Duncan Stewart et al., "The Cloud Migration Forecast: Cloudy with a Chance of Clouds," Deloitte, December 7, 2020, *https://oreil.ly/nE39X*.

10 "Top 7 Trends Shaping Digital Transformation in 2022," MuleSoft, *https://oreil.ly/SnEf8*.

11 F5, "The State of Application Strategy in 2022."

12 Cameron Gain, "How OpenTelemetry Can Serve as Observability's Missing On-Ramp," The New Stack, January 21, 2021, *https://oreil.ly/xP2tR*.

Similar normalization efforts are occurring in the industry for infrastructure and environments, led by the broad adoption of the eponymously named open telemetry standard, OpenTelemetry (*https://oreil.ly/4yE4P*). A robust set of service and product companies such as GitHub, F5, Splunk, Google, Microsoft, and more have embraced the need for interoperable telemetry and adopted this standard, paving the way for technology leaders to normalize telemetry across applications, infrastructure, environments, and third-party services.

This shift recognizes that raw data has no value. In the case of telemetry, the value is in uncovering patterns and relationships that produce insights about the performance and security of the digital experience. In the industry, this will drive differentiation through analytics. For businesses and technology leaders, the same opportunity for competitive advantage is derived from the ability to analyze telemetry in near-real time and proactively address conditions that have the potential to negatively impact the customer experience.

Application telemetry allows an enterprise to track many performance data points across services, infrastructure, and the network, as shown in Figure 6-6. In particular, note how many services the CheckoutService depends on. A performance degradation or failure in any of these services can cause the Check outService to become slow or unresponsive. The customer, seeing only an unresponsive user interface, may become frustrated and abandon the transaction, resulting in the loss of potential revenue to the business. Tracking the performance of each application helps determine whether the overall system is running smoothly, how it is being used, and who is using it. All this information can be compiled into dashboards and reports that are made available to stakeholders of the system, application, or business. On top of providing real-time performance data, data can also be collected at different time intervals to identify any patterns. This information can be priceless when coupled with customer (business) data.

The classic example of this relationship is Amazon's discovery, more than a decade ago, that even 100 ms of latency was responsible for the loss of 1% in sales.[13] Understanding the connection between technology and business results is a key capability for a digital business.

---

13 Yoav Einav, "Amazon Found Every 100ms of Latency Cost Them 1% in Sales," GigaSpaces, January 20, 2019, *https://oreil.ly/9MNNw*.

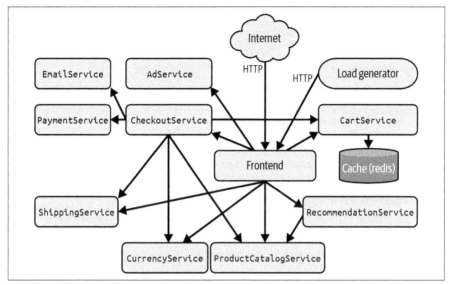

Figure 6-6. Every service and system must be instrumented to ensure accurate analysis

As we move into this telemetry and automation age, the challenge is sometimes not in producing data, collecting data, or scaling, but in predicting whether the data measured will be useful or impactful to the overall state of the system, user experience, etc. This is where AI and the subfield ML become relevant; we talk about this later in the section. That stated, no automation, predictions, or great analytics can be performed without data (telemetry).

Telemetry is critical to our multicloud infrastructures and systems. It is no longer acceptable for vendor products to manipulate, aggregate, be opinionated (sums, averages, etc.), or even hold data hostage from the enterprise. Business decisions from application development, system performance, user adoption, user experience, and more depend on the granularity and verbosity of the telemetry within these systems. We talk about managing that data in the next section; however, at the time of writing, this problem—ingestion, scaling pipelines, and data storage and management—has been solved for more than five years at scale.

Telemetry Collection and Management

Since every industry is adopting and leveraging telemetry-based technologies such as automation to operate more efficiently and increase productivity, we should understand how to establish a scalable telemetry practice. When observing a digital business, we must think about many different data sets. Normalizing them to be analyzed in real time and at scale is a significant challenge. Companies that want to compete in the future need to figure out how to manage telemetry at scale in ways that will generate intelligence and fuel their business.

Data Lake: A Modern Approach to Storing Data

A key difference between storing data in a digital business and in a traditional business is the need for flexibility in the way the data will be consumed and analyzed. Data warehouses are the norm in traditional businesses, with well-defined use cases for the data that drive its structure. A digital business needs telemetry for real-time analysis, forecasting, modeling, and historical comparisons. These approaches require different technology and structures. Thus, the modern approach to storing and scaling operational data is establishing a data lake. The core difference is in the way data is stored; in a data warehouse, data is normalized and highly structured, while in a data lake, the data is often normalized but raw. This approach enables a more robust set of tools and use cases and allows for adaptation when new uses arise.

Chapter 4 provides a more thorough discussion of data management and governance. Here we need to look at a key factor peculiar to managing telemetry: latency. This results from the way telemetry is used in digital business to drive operational decisions. Telemetry must often be collected, processed, and analyzed, and must produce a result in split-second time to be of value. Because the human brain can process only 60 bits per second, we must look for a programmatic approach that includes automating actions produced by this process.

This is especially true in industries where the health and safety of human beings requires fast responses based on rapid—and accurate—analysis of massive amounts of data. In these cases, collecting, storing, analyzing, and producing an action must be accomplished within milliseconds. For example, smart healthcare devices demand less than 1 ms of end-to-end latency.[14] This requires an

---

14 Andressa Vergütz et al., "An Architecture for the Performance Management of Smart Healthcare Applications," *Sensors* 20, no. 19 (September 28, 2020): 5566.

automated telemetry pipeline, from generation to ingestion to normalization and processing. There is no room for human intervention when milliseconds matter.

This leads to the perception—or misperception—of where data should be managed. This has led to many debates over the years, as data collection systems and management of that data is often discussed in terms of cost-effectiveness or performance across a system or network.

For modern enterprises, this problem becomes easier to address. Most businesses do not have to meet such stringent requirements with respect to latency. A reasonable expectation can be stated as "Digital services must respond within the blink of an eye." That sounds blazingly quick, but the reality is that the average blink of an eye is between 100 and 150 ms. With the advances of new data storage and management systems within public cloud infrastructures and open source tooling, this is fairly easy to achieve at a reasonable cost. The average cost in 2022 for typical storage is roughly $.020 per gigabyte/month. This can be further optimized for cold storage at around $.0012 per GB/month. Latency problems still might exist, even if full automation is employed, but can be addressed or normalized by the application stack, CDNs, or the use of edge computing. If full automation is not employed, managing data latency is, in effect, the capability of an operator to respond to a data point, which is well beyond seconds and more likely within minutes.

If a process is not automated completely (i.e., if one step is manual), it is fair to state that the digital business is only as fast as the slowest process interval. If that process involves a human, latency when managing data is not the highest priority.

It turns out cost and latency are not as big of an issue for management, as the combination of public clouds and open source have solved for much of this.

Automation and Orchestration

With the rise in popularity of AI, automation and orchestration software has changed the world of computing and accelerated the pace of digital transformation toward its destination: digital business. Three out of four C-suite executives believe that if they don't scale AI in the next five years, they risk going out of business entirely.[15]

---

15 Athena Reilly et al., "AI: Built to Scale," Accenture, November 14, 2019, *https://oreil.ly/IjRBC*.

The final phase of digital transformation is the use of AI to make more strategic decisions faster. For technology leaders, this requires a focus on the data, analytics, and automation needed to support it across all areas of IT and the business. While most organizations will already have a strong foundation in data and analytics, leveraging operational data (telemetry) and automation will require new team structures, practices, and tooling. This is why both observability and automation are included as new domains within the digital enterprise architecture. Both imply capabilities, technology, and skill sets that are not represented in traditional architecture frameworks.

WHAT IS AUTOMATION?

Automation has been a buzzword for a long time. We see many tools that help enterprises automate repetitive tasks, such as Ansible, Terraform, and Python, to name a few. But what really is automation?

From the industrial revolution to self-driving cars, automation has always been a huge part of our lives. Telemetry and automation have been intertwined for many years now, with telemetry driving automation to operate infrastructure, services, devices, etc. A signal is determined, and an action is executed (or not) to ensure the expected state of a system. We can draw analogies from the stock market, aerospace, electric vehicles, healthcare, and manufacturing industries, where automated actions are taken based on telemetry every second of the day.

Automation in the context of digital business is more than using tools to automate a task. Automation in a digital business is about recognizing system inefficiency through telemetry and making programmatic changes to the system to achieve a sustainable objective, e.g., 99.99% uptime or <=100 ms of latency per request. Without SLOs, automation is limited to reducing manual or repetitive activities. Inefficiency of troubleshooting—root cause analysis—is also addressable by a combination of telemetry, analytics, and automation. Of the top three insights that technology leaders are missing, root cause analysis occupies two spots: one for outages and the other for performance degradation.[16] Lack of visibility—metrics—is a key factor driving root-cause diagnosis to consume 72% of the average three-hour mean time to repair (MTTR) in most organizations.[17]

---

16 F5, "The State of Application Strategy in 2022."

17 Deepak Jannu, "The Roadmap to Becoming a Top Performing IT Operations Organization," OpsRamp, September 12, 2019, *https://oreil.ly/qiKyd.*

While it is important to adopt automation to address system inefficiencies, it is also important to recognize that the workforce is hard pressed to keep up with the ever-changing landscape and stay competitive, especially when faced with an accelerated rate of digital transformation. Therefore, we must use automation to shift the burden of day-to-day operations from people to technology. Automation can eliminate time waste, optimize investments, and increase productivity. This is accomplished most effectively when well-designed operational plans such as methods of procedure (MOPs) are built and testing is done frequently to adapt for system changes. What automation is *not* is a fix for a bad application, system, or infrastructure design, or inefficient processes. In fact, automating inefficient processes simply hides the root cause and prevents addressing the problem.

Automation is also a critical component of a successful shift toward SRE operations. Automation is more than a means to shift the burden of manual activities from people to technology to achieve scale. It also provides the opportunity to optimize workflows that require human intervention, such as tuning operations to meet business outcomes and reduce lag time between incidents and alerts. Automation can be used to quickly deliver insights to the right people to decrease MTTR and improve customer and employee experiences.

THE RELATIONSHIP BETWEEN OBSERVABILITY AND AUTOMATION

Observability provides the metrics, and automation the means, to either remediate or deliver actionable plans to the right people. As discussed in Chapter 4 with respect to data, a strategy is required to successfully execute on observability and automation initiatives. A well-defined strategy will be the difference between surviving in a digital economy and thriving. Simply focusing on traditional objectives for automation will not net organizations the benefits of adaptability. Objectives must be aligned with business outcomes to yield a significant return on investment.

While AI and ML are capable of producing operational insights and uncovering business opportunities, without automation, human beings are still required to act upon them. One of the most common examples of operational automation is autoscaling of applications in response to demand.

Note

The relationship between automation and telemetry can be understood by the impact of metrics that feed autoscaling algorithms. The problem of selecting the right metrics to optimize activation of autoscaling is a challenge many are trying to solve.[18] An assumption exists that if you have access to a wide range of metrics, the organization has enabled observability across all systems.

Few organizations today consider it risky or odd for an automated process to autoscale applications. Yet this capability has come into widespread use only in the last decade. Similarly, the use of automation to detect and neutralize attacks and bad actors (bots) is nearly a requirement today for security services and products.

Similar capabilities to adjust configuration and policies across all infrastructure and application security and delivery services will quickly evolve to meet the challenge required to scale operations in a digital business. These kinds of "auto-operations" are foundational to implementing the real-time digital operations approach that most (69%) technology leaders need to shift the balance away from tackling digital incidents to innovation.[19]

The use of automation can alleviate the burden on human operators and offer the time necessary to develop innovative plans and strategies that take advantage of newly discovered insights. It can be said that automation makes the operation of a digital business more efficient, thereby freeing people to focus on innovation. Organizations that have embraced automation benefit from improved consistency, speed, and scalability of business processes with some reaping time savings of 70%.[20]

Automation and orchestration can be used in various tasks, from simple data processing to complex data crunching, to develop automated program execution. It is worth calling out a significant delta between automation and orchestration. *Automation* is task oriented, typically done to remove repetitive activities that easily could be performed by a tool, script, or software. *Orchestration* is about automating multiple tasks together, not a single task but an

---

18 Emiliano Casalicchio and Vanessa Perciballi, "Auto-Scaling of Containers: The Impact of Relative and Absolute Metrics," *2017 IEEE 2nd International Workshops on Foundations and Applications of Self* Systems* (2017): 207–214.

19 Vivian Chan, "New Tech Leader Survey Reveals Why The Time for Real-Time Operations Is Now," PagerDuty, November 10, 2021, *https://oreil.ly/5bQMj*.

20 "What Is Artificial Intelligence?," Accenture, accessed May 30, 2022, *https://oreil.ly/XyFBC*.

entire process. Orchestration is not just a task-automation tool but a process-automation capability.

Note

Consider application development and, in particular, the way in which development lifecycles are increasingly orchestrated via continuous integration and continuous delivery (CI/CD) pipelines. Organizations adopting automation of the development lifecycle report benefits of faster release rates, improved code quality, and detection of defects earlier in the lifecycle.[21] But these benefits apply to a fully orchestrated development process. Even a single task requiring manual intervention will negatively impact the release rate and can introduce new defects. For decades, automation has been used in traditional enterprise environments to facilitate portions of the development lifecycle. *Makefiles* are good examples of task automation. Makefiles were capable of including very basic automation to execute a build task for software. CI/CD introduced and emphasizes *orchestration* of the entire process, not just the build or test. CI/CD automation enables scale and speed but more importantly introduces the consistency and repeatability necessary to produce quality software.

Conclusion

In general, you should view the need for automation as the means and methods to remove frequent manual activities, e.g., upgrading, adding, moving, changing, etc. However, that does not mean you must automate everything. A lot of activities should not be and are not automated. It is a tough balance at times; however, simple evaluation steps can quantify whether something should be automated:

Frequency
How often is this performed?

Time
How long does it take to perform?

Reliability
Is there a risk of human error?

Consistency
Can this be done repeatedly?

---

21 "State of CI/CD Survey 2020," ActiveState, *https://oreil.ly/GrcEu*.

Cost

What is the measurement of the outcome?

One of the best reads in the automation domain is found in Chapter 7 of *Site Reliability Engineering* (O'Reilly), edited by Betsy Beyer et al.: "The Evolution of Automation at Google." It is a must read for those who want to do a deeper dive into building an automation framework.

A burgeoning automation tooling market strives to keep the promises of optimization, efficiencies, and time savings. Given the increasing complexity of cloud systems and applications today, more time should be spent on developing orchestration tooling that can interface with many APIs to achieve business objectives.

Technology leaders should strive to optimize meeting business objectives. Care should be taken not to automate expensive actions without guardrails, nor codify inefficient processes. If you modernize architecture with that in mind, rather than just making operators more productive, you will achieve greater success.

The Need for Speed

—Julia Renouard, F5 VP of Engineering

Dotting the landscape of the world's highways and freeways are signs declaring the speed limit. While these limits vary based on geography, population density, and from country to country, there exists an underlying shared concept that speed controls correlate with safety.

Just 10 years ago, enterprises were built on organizational assumptions that inherently gated delivery of new software and systems under the principle of ensuring system integrity and uptime. It was, in fact, necessary. Our traditional systems were more monolithic, limited in scale. All functionality was knit together in a more highly coupled system. You could not update one component without impacting the whole. To ensure system integrity and meet commitments to SLAs, technology leaders dedicated teams to focus on operating these IT systems. The world of software operated at a slower pace, and no less on the consumer side. Users were limited in their options; with perpetual licensing models, data-center-focused deployments, and more complex integrations, the cost to change was higher.

A lot has changed in 10 years. With the birth of the public cloud has come a revolution in the way we deliver applications. Cloud-native architectural models and a mesh of loosely coupled, interconnected services provide ready-to-consume building blocks that unleash the ability for modern enterprises to experiment and accelerate at a pace never before experienced. With this has come a fast-paced landscape of consumer-ready apps and digital services whose cost to change is low, and user experience reigns supreme. Enterprises built on the models of prior decades must fundamentally shift to keep up with the expectations and challenges of this accelerating digital world. The organizational models and assumptions of prior generations are no longer sufficient to catch up or keep up with the new digital enterprise.

So, where is the problem? A traditional business relies on a stack of IT technologies and organizational structures that are mostly static and monolithic. Built on manual processes and siloed teams, this inherently limits the ability to scale and manage quality and reliability. It also limits the ability to adapt quickly to changes in demand, market pressures, or threats. Furthermore, manual processes also limit the complexity of the system. Absorbing the complexity introduced by the hybrid cloud, microservices, the edge, and APIs without adopting new processes and ways of working leaves organizations struggling to modernize and keep up. F5 CTO Geng Lin says this:

> Compare booking a taxi before 2010 to booking a Lyft or Uber today— you're still hiring someone to drive you from one place to another. But now that service is offered in a way that is automated and flexible and adapts to changes in demand without a human operator in the middle. The traditional taxi service must anticipate demand well in advance and plan for capacity. It is a manual staffing and planning exercise that is self-limiting. Services such as Uber build in mechanisms to expand capacity more dynamically as demand increases. This is done automatically, with no human intervention, save for the "app" reacting to the data.

The traditional enterprise architecture is *just as outdated* as phoning for a taxi. That's because the traditional IT operating model was not designed for cloud technologies and distributed architectures. It was not designed for the growing challenge of observing and responding to complex systems, nor was it designed to scale without significant reliance on human operators.

Business leaders are not unaware of the challenges they face in modernizing IT to meet the needs of a fully digital business. They lack a clear roadmap that guides them from where they are today to where they need to be to operate as a digital enterprise. The changes required impact more than organizational structure or tooling. IT requires a fundamental shift in the mindset of business and IT to adopt new practices that are designed to excel in a data-driven, real-time digital world. Today, those practices can be summed up by the principles behind SRE. These practices are more than a set of guiding principles; they are a new approach to operating digital businesses that span the use of data, modernization of tooling, automation, and providing the guardrails necessary for the critical human component to operate in a scalable, safe, and fast-paced environment.

It is no surprise that 83% of corporations believe that they need to modernize their operations and adopt SRE practices.[1] SRE is the bridge that connects observability (data) and automation, and ensures that both serve to fulfill business and customer expectations, as described in Chapter 6.

SRE is a key capability in an enterprise architecture for digital business, but this does not mean human decision making and judgment is eliminated. In fact, through SRE practices, we allow humans to offload the rote and repeatable operations and focus on what they do best. This is especially true in industries where the wrong decision may put human safety and well-being at risk:

Human judgment plays a role throughout a seemingly objective system of logical decisions. Humans write algorithms, define success or failure, and make decisions about the uses of systems and who may be affected by a system's outcomes.[2]

But as noted in Chapter 3, relying on human operators does not scale and introduces challenges with communication that impede speed of delivery, deployment quality, and consistency. Technology provides the means by which organizations can scale human capacity and more effectively apply their judgment across a wide variety of operational tasks and make more strategic decisions.

A digital business, operating on a global scale, can generate millions or even billions of digital signals per second. Each one must be analyzed—in context—and sense made of the information it represents. Simple HTTP errors could be site dead ends or abandoned shopping carts. Lost customers could be hidden in higher latency. But this process only provides the *what* that is happening in a digital business. It does not answer the question, "What do we do about it?" This is the realm of human expertise that ultimately guides and even teaches the systems responsible for automation to act in accordance with human judgment. This is the role of SRE within a modern enterprise architecture.

Adopting SRE is more than simply changing titles and hiring new talent. It requires new practices, tools, and, perhaps most difficult of all, a shift in mindset and culture.

This chapter explores SRE practices, tools, and culture—and the intersection with DevOps—to provide leaders with a more comprehensive understanding of

1 "The State of Application Strategy in 2022," F5, April 12, 2022, *https://oreil.ly/vyab6*.
2 IBM, "Accountability," IBM Design for AI, May 2019, *https://oreil.ly/jcvFx*.

the need for, and benefits of, SRE operations in driving the modernization of their operations and accelerating value in a digital world.

The Shift to SRE

Why do you need SRE? Why don't traditional methods and architectures work? To understand why SRE was born, we need to more deeply examine the fundamental shift in realities that modern digital architectures bring. The problem can be summed up with two words: *complexity* and *speed*.

Modern architectures deliver an increasing number of benefits that enterprises can no longer ignore. The public cloud provides stability and elastic scale that technology leaders simply cannot replicate quickly or cost-effectively. A microservice architecture allows you to upgrade components or add new value more easily than the monolithic architectures ever could. Controlled A/B experiments are suddenly a possibility, giving you faster customer feedback on changes. Edge technology innovations allow you to distribute these components in ways that optimize the user experience and continue to offer new scaling opportunities.

Enterprises recognize now more than ever the imperative to transform. A majority (91%) of large enterprises believe their traditional architectures are no longer able to meet the challenges of the digital era.[3] Going even further, 71% of IT decision makers are looking to AI to help address security challenges.[4] Another 65% are planning to adopt modern real-time digital operations with a goal to accelerate innovation in their business.[5] These surveys are showing a remarkable trend; they are detecting the unexpected accelerant to transformation brought by the COVID-19 pandemic, which forced a level of transformation in 12 months we would not have otherwise seen in 10 years. In 2021, a surprising 94% of respondents had increased their focus on SRE in the past year.[6] Preexisting inefficiencies became existential business risks as many organizations flipped overnight to work entirely from home. The need to automate was no longer a nice-to-have.

All this comes at a cost: complexity. The challenges for traditional service operations teams climb exponentially with the level of complexity introduced by

---

3 "2021: The Year Real-Time Operations Got Real," PagerDuty, 2022, *https://oreil.ly/1xCzF*.

4 F5, "The State of Application Strategy in 2022."

5 PagerDuty, "2021: The Year Real-Time Operations Got Real."

6 Jessica Abelson, "State of DevOps Automation 2021 Report Reveals Automation Holds the Key to Scaling Reliably," Transposit, April 6, 2021, *https://oreil.ly/rwtpD*.

modern architectures. With a mesh of connections, multiple clouds, providers, tools, and failure points, the system can no longer simply be managed through traditional practices, tools, or organizational structures. It requires new tools and methods so you can take advantage of the continuously evolving marketplace of digital services and accelerate your delivery of value to your customers.

In fact, this becomes a business imperative, not just an optimization. Organizational agility is an essential business attribute. Resilience in the face of uncertainty and change allows a business not just to survive but to thrive. Organizational agility allows you to pivot, adopt new technologies, learn from failures, and identify new opportunities. Speed is another imperative. Lock-in of users is no longer assumed as the friction to change has been lowered. You retain users by ensuring that their experience is good, getting the value they expect, and constantly delivering new value.

SRE brings in practices that allow you to manage this complexity: monitoring, reducing toil through automation, using tools to understand system reliability and performance, adopting a continuous improvement mindset, and encouraging a cultural shift that reduces siloing to improve delivery outcomes. Through this, SRE practices enable you to adapt to a changing world, increase reliability and speed, and manage the mounting complexity while realizing the advantages offered in the ever-evolving world of digital services.

HOW DO WE KNOW THIS IS EFFECTIVE?

The old rules of speed and safety fly out the window, and we're left with a seeming paradox: how can we increase speed and safety while driving efficiency? Isn't there an inherent tension between reliability and speed? The fact is, we can increase both reliability and speed and deliver world-class results. Let's look at some industry data.

Over the past 10 years, a cross section of industry professionals has collaborated on surveying, researching, and measuring practices correlated with high-performance companies. The DevOps Research and Assessment (DORA) State of DevOps research reports (*https://oreil.ly/EJV6s*) are a series of annual reports seeking to identify the key factors in high-performing organizations.

As shown in Figure 7-1, the "State of DevOps 2021" report focuses on five top-level metrics that are strong indicators of high-performing organizations: *lead time* and *deployment frequency* measure speed of delivery, *change failure rates* and *time to restore service* measure resiliency to failure, and *reliability* is essentially the organization's ability to fulfill its promises about the services it provides.

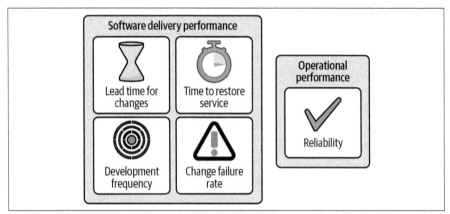

Figure 7-1. Key metrics from the "State of DevOps 2021" DORA report (https://oreil.ly/PSHoM)

The consistent findings are that organizations that can reduce failures can also increase speed of delivery. "Teams that prioritize both delivery and operational excellence report the highest organizational performance."[7] Further, the DORA research shows that organizations demonstrating more maturity in SRE practices were 1.8 times more likely to report better business outcomes. This has been replicated and reinforced year after year.

Adopting SRE practices isn't only about the speed of delivery and reliability. This is also about the agility of the system to embrace and adopt the growing advances in technology and services that also expand our ability to deliver new value. Can we do this as well? As it turns out, research also shows a high correlation between the adoption of SRE practices and the ability to embrace emerging technology.[8]

Table 7-1 illustrates this correlation by comparing the percentage of organizations that have adopted SRE versus those that have not against the adoption of modern and emerging technologies. For example, adoption of multicloud infrastructure and the use of AI across IT and business functions is far more likely in organizations that have adopted SRE practices versus those organizations that have not. While the adoption of early edge computing technologies such as CDNs (Edge 1.0) is not affected by the adoption of SRE, latter evolutions of edge such as security as a service (Edge 1.5) and application and data workload distribution (Edge 2.0) are impacted. This strong correlation indicates that

---

7 DORA, "Accelerate: State of DevOps 2021," Google Cloud, *https://oreil.ly/PSHOM*.

8 F5, "The State of Application Strategy in 2022."

the practices and approaches associated with SRE are well suited to embracing emerging technologies in early stages, implying a greater capacity to innovate.

Table 7-1. SRE adoption is a strong indicator of early technology adoption

Workloads planned at the edge	Have adopted SRE	Have not adopted SRE
Edge 1 (caching, mirror, etc.)	48%	48%
Edge 1.5 (security as a service)	61%	47%
Edge 2.0 (data/app distribution)	84%	66%
Repatriation		
Repatriated apps from public cloud	87%	7%
Multicloud		
Have apps in multiple clouds	97%	32%
Plan/use AI		
Business	74%	40%
Operations	49%	34%
Security	73%	44%

As it turns out, speed versus safety is actually not a paradox; it is a virtuous feedback loop enabled by SRE. Improving how well you recover from failure and minimizing the cost of failure enables acceleration in deployment frequency and reduces lead time in delivering value. Additionally, these practices increase the agility of our enterprise to embrace new technologies at a faster rate. And all of this results in improvements in the availability of your services and applications while simultaneously accelerating growth.

WHY 5 × 9S IS NO LONGER ENOUGH

The world of IT should be familiar with the concept of 5 × 9s. For the uninitiated, this is an expression of uptime as 99.999% of the time (thus 5 × 9s). This was a standard held by the telecommunications industry of yesteryear and by critical systems across industry categories. It was a recognition of the criticality of certain services that people and the industry relied on for constant availability. This standard itself required that these operations teams be extremely careful. Breaking this contract could trigger regulatory or SLA breach penalties, beyond just the obligation for critical services such as the telephone and emergency services. These requirements and necessary ways of working reinforced the siloed organization of traditional IT.

In simpler times with monolithic systems, uptime was a useful concept. It was easy to measure and strongly correlated with the user experience and availability of the service. But applications today are not a single component. They are a complex web of services—authentication, security, CDN, data and storage, frontend, mobile, or web. Components are distributed across data center, SaaS, and edge. There is no simple measure of uptime in a modern architecture. The increasing complexity of these systems means an exponential increase in the ways even subtle changes can impact system performance and reliability. Any one failure, however seemingly benign, can have unintended consequences. Even simple changes could have a cascading effect in your system. An API that changes its response time from 100 ms to 200 ms, when called millions of times, can result in timeouts that cascade into failures. So how do you measure reliability? What does uptime mean anymore?

First, let's define *reliability*. The "State of DevOps 2021" defines reliability as "the degree to which a team can keep promises and assertions about the software they operate." How do we measure and quantify our promises? At this point, it is useful to dig in and look at the tools to understand this. To do so, let's review a few terms:

Service-level agreements (SLAs)
This should be a familiar concept in IT. This is a contractual agreement with your customers on high-level measures of system performance. An SLA is often associated with financial commitments, and as such these are very high-level promises. Examples are a response to a support incident in one hour or having fewer than four outages per year.

Service-level objectives (SLOs)
SLOs are more nuanced. These are not contractual commitments; they are measures of system performance objectives that usually represent a key measurable aspect of user experience. Examples include response time on your application or website, latency on API calls, system availability, and download time. The service may be external and customer facing, or internal only (such as an authentication service or a database). SLOs are higher-level objectives set from more granular indicator metrics that help you understand the multiple variables in a complex system. SLOs are also the measure by which you set users' expectations. While not contractual (that is, we're not committing to a penalty), these are the promises we're making to our users and business partners as to what their experience will be.

Service-level indicators (SLIs)

SLIs are more detailed indicator metrics, and this is where the art of the SRE really comes into play. SLIs are the current state measures. These are what you use to determine whether you're meeting your objectives. The art of the SLI is in determining which indicators to use and how to measure them. Finer-grained measures such as latency and error rates in key areas of the system can give you a better indication of how the system is performing. But the *how* matters. Factors such as sampling and averaging also play a role in how meaningful your measurements are.

You may have noticed we're talking about reliability, not availability. What is the difference? Why isn't a 5 × 9s target desirable? Isn't 100% uptime always the goal?

First, let's understand what 5 × 9s of availability actually means: 24 hours × 365 days = 8,760 hours. So 99.999% uptime allows for 5.3 minutes of downtime *per year*. Yes, some critical services need this level of availability, but most day-to-day services can tolerate some minor hiccups without the user noticing. Your human resource management (HRM) system can have a planned outage of many hours quarterly without significantly impacting business workflows. Most user-based systems can tolerate a five-second hiccup now and again, and users won't notice.

On the other hand, emergency communications and public safety systems should have extremely high availability requirements. You also need to examine the services within your mesh of services. Backend services, such as database systems, require more robust and consistent reliability, or the dependent services will backlog and potentially result in cascading failures.

The key to recognize is that the cost for each additional 9 can be exponentially more expensive, depending on the service, but may not bring the same level of additional user value. Further, unnecessary and overly aggressive uptime objectives can have the unintended consequence of slowing your organization by limiting or making changes unreasonably burdensome. Another potentially surprising cost of overly ambitious reliability goals may be dependencies with unrealistic expectations. Since any service's reliability will be a function of the reliability of its dependent services, attention should be paid to setting expectations that are realistic and reasonable. Google shares that it deliberately introduces failures into a backend system to ensure that the cascade of downstream dependent services are designed to expect failures, thus ensuring that those dependent services can expect and mitigate failures in a way to meet their own SLOs.[9]

A surprising finding is that lowering the cost of failure is often better than eliminating failure. Setting an expectation of no failures constrains your agility and speed, but creating a system that is resilient—and in which risk is well managed to not impact user experience—unleashes agility and speed.

Setting the right level of reliability for your service is something you need to decide, but the cost of setting this value too high is not just slowing your organization but also investing in the wrong thing. Your goal should be to set SLO targets low enough that you're not impacting customer value, allowing you to maximize the speed of new value and organizational agility. On the other hand, SLOs also provide a useful way to determine when you may need to tip the scales toward investing in reliability over new features. If you're not meeting your SLOs, stopping new feature development while you stabilize the system may be the right move. Sometimes you have to slow down to speed up, and SLOs can be an indicator you use to help make that decision.

What Is SRE Operations?

We've established the benefits and discussed the research. Now let's understand what *SRE* really means. In the increasingly complex digital ecosystems in which technology leaders find themselves, you need to balance increasing delivery speed while understanding and retaining the quality of experience that users and the business demands. This requires a new approach.

SRE is the newest field of engineering and has seen strong growth, adoption, and maturing science since it was introduced by Google in the early 2000s. Despite existing for more than 20 years, the population of SRE-skilled professionals remains low, estimated at just under 7,000 practitioners in the US in 2021.[10] The US Bureau of Labor Statistics estimates a 9% projected job growth for site reliability engineers through 2024.

When compared to the estimated 350,000 traditional system administrator roles responsible for operations, SRE roles appear anemic.[11] This is because SRE

9 Betsy Beyer et al., *Site Reliability Engineering* (Sebastopol, CA: O'Reilly, 2016), *https://oreil.ly/YuurQ*.

10 "Reliability Engineer Demographics and Statistics in the US," Zippia, accessed May 30, 2022, *https://oreil.ly/1JMgF*.

11 "Occupational Outlook Handbook," US Bureau of Labor Statistics, accessed May 30, 2022, *https://oreil.ly/tLKyq*.

is not just a set of processes, practices, and tools; it is also a mindset shift. It brings a new understanding to the meaning of *reliability*, a mindset that seeks to manage complexity and risk, and a Lean philosophy and practice that measures value and reduces "toil" and waste, with continuous improvement built in.

One goal for SRE is to automate and instrument a system in such a way that you can manage complexity effectively and ensure resiliency of an increasingly complex system. The other goal is to provide the guardrails developers need to allow them to ensure that their changes are not compromising system integrity and reliability. The more gates and barriers we can remove, the more reliability we can build into the system, and the faster we can deploy and add business value day by day. The key is managing risk. We're not trying to eliminate risk but rather to lower the cost of failures. This is the key to unlocking speed.

Adopting SRE should be an important part of your strategy to modernize IT and operate as a digital business. It is critical to achieving the organizational agility needed to scale safely at speed. SRE gives you the tools to:

- Understand what reliability and performance mean to customers/users (SLOs)

- Increase the agility of your teams to deliver new business value (speed of delivery)

- Drive operational efficiency and service reliability (automation and best practices)

The Tools and Practice of SRE

The practices of yesterday's IT separated development and operations teams. Developers would develop and test, then throw it over the wall to the operations team to deploy, manage, and secure. This required a series of gates and processes for software to be deployed successfully. Operations was expected to put the brakes on developers as they owned the system reliability. In the best case, you could deploy new changes in months.

SRE changes this paradigm by removing the walls between development and operations, instrumenting the system to ensure integrity and quality and allow high-performing organizations to deploy many times a day, and implementing high-reliability measures. So how does SRE do that?

As previously mentioned, SRE is a set of practices that focus on system and site reliability. Instead of just measuring uptime, it measures the level of service. Operational data (telemetry) is the core asset, gleaned through instrumented systems. An SRE uses telemetry to predict failures and measure the service level of the system in a more meaningful way than the traditional measures of uptime.

Core SRE principles include the following:

Monitoring health

Instrumenting and monitoring key aspects of your system's health and availability allows you to understand long-term trends, compare and experiment the impact of changes, alert and proactively detect failures, and conduct more data-driven retrospective analysis.

Measuring service levels

SLOs are an aggregate view of the system's performance to represent the level of service, ideally representing the experience of your users. It is also a vehicle to set expectations, allowing you to set a safety margin (tolerance for failures) and not overinvest in service levels that don't matter.

Eliminating toil

Eliminating manual, repetitive, low-value or tactical tasks with automation allows you to invest in people who create new value through innovation. Manual toil is the top challenge during remediation, with 51.7% of respondents reporting that a lack of automation is preventing them from quickly taking action to resolve an incident.[12]

Stabilizing the core and innovating at the edges

Automation and quality checks help developers deliver new value that won't impact core stability. As you evolve your system, you will start to identify those core foundational components that are key to stability, have less need for frequent change, and can be abstracted out as a service. This allows the development of new value to be thoroughly decoupled and deployed in its own cadence, with lower-cost impact of failures.

---

12 DORA, "Accelerate: State of DevOps 2021."

These principles are enabled by a robust set of practices and tools, many of which are available through open source:

Data and observability

Monitor and measure everything you can. Health, performance, latency, quality, and error rates are typical sentinel measures. The open source world is rich with tools such as Prometheus and Grafana, as well as standards such as OpenTelemetry.

Automation and tooling

Anything you can automate—system delivery and deployment, quality checks, manual tasks, remediation, and system recovery—will help you to build more resiliency and improve speed of deployment. Again, the open source community has a wealth of options that are continuously evolving and improving. This includes treating infrastructure as code. Treating your infrastructure as code provides another quality check and change control rigor, raising the bar on service-level quality. Tools such as Ansible, ArgoCD and Terraform, and Helm and Porter are part of the rich set of tooling available to speed your own automation journey.

Continuous improvement

A complex system is never static. We need a process of continuous examination of failures and issues to understand how they can be improved. This feedback loop drives the system on the continuous path of automation and efficiency, allowing systems to self-manage and self-heal as their maturity improves.

Like DevOps, SRE is a mindset that is rooted in well-established industry Agile and Lean practices. But while DevOps is about increasing the quality, security, and velocity of development and deployments, SRE focuses on increasing the system's reliability, performance, resiliency, and efficiency. Both are essential to maintaining and increasing reliability of a system while increasing the speed of deployment.

Getting Started

How do you get started on your SRE journey? While existing tomes offer fantastic examples dedicated to the practice in detail, this section provides you with a high-level roadmap. To get started with SRE, we recommend three basic actions:

- Start measuring.
  — Identify your top two to three SLOs; identify measurable objectives that are meaningful to the user.
  — Instrument your system for data and monitor and track it over time; keep it simple to start.
- Start automating.
  — Identify the top opportunities to reduce manual steps.
  — Identify the top areas in which automation would improve quality.
  — Identify how automation can prevent or remediate degradations or failures.
- Start improving.
  — Implement a continuous improvement system. What events are impacting your users or are of higher cost for you? Where can you augment and improve? Wash, rinse, repeat.

The rest of this section expands on each of these actions in more detail.

START MEASURING

Without monitoring, you have no way to know how the system is actually performing and will have no data for analysis when something goes wrong. Of course, you cannot just monitor a system blindly; you need to decide what to monitor and then instrument it for monitoring, as discussed in Chapter 6. A wealth of tools are out there—open source and commercial, with new tools coming to market every day. We'll leave that as your homework. Getting basic data collection in place first is essential, as it gives you a baseline from which to understand any other changes. The following is the approach.

Identify your top two to three SLOs

First you need to identify what your users care about. Pick one or two key performance objectives that you strongly believe most represent your users' experience and that you can actually measure.[13] Do not base those objectives on current performance and give yourself a reasonable bar for errors. For example, if you're measuring file-transfer times, you know you will see some natural variability.

---

13 Beyer et al., *Site Reliability Engineering*.

Setting your upper bound too low will cause over-alerting, but you also want to know when it becomes consistently longer than users expect or will tolerate.

You also don't want to be overly aggressive, beyond where there is value. A one-second download time would be great, but users may expect downloads to take a few seconds if the files are large. If we know users can easily tolerate up to 10 seconds, energy invested in further improvement may start hitting the inflection point of marginal utility. That same effort may be better invested in new capabilities or value.

Instrument for data and monitoring

An SRE without data is like a pilot without a compass: you're flying blind. Data and monitoring are critical tools. Do you have your systems instrumented in a way that you can monitor and measure key indicators and your SLOs over time? And just as important, are they instrumented in a way that does not negatively affect system performance? Further, you need to understand how you're measuring and interpreting the data to extrapolate meaningful results. Can you see the signals correlated to reduced reliability and service levels or as indicators of impending outages?

The "four golden signals" are latency, traffic, errors, and saturation.[14] While not universal, these four basic measures are good starting indicators that will help you begin your data journey.

Your SLO is your goal. Your SLI is your actual measure. If your SLO is 99.9% availability, you may start by measuring HTTP 200 responses and latency less than 500 ms. If 10 requests out of 100,00 exceed the 500 ms latency, that is 99.9%. As long as both SLIs are within SLO targets, you are meeting your SLOs.

Building up your historical data will also give you a better sense of your performance over time. SLOs allow you to create meaningful proxy measures of your users' experience while giving you realistic targets for what reliability means.

START AUTOMATING

Automation is one of the key tools of an SRE practice. Automation has three key goals: quality, reduced toil, and resiliency.

---

14 Ibid.

Automate quality and security

Test automation is just as much a friend of SRE as it is to DevOps. Test automation in your CI/CD pipelines helps you ensure that your system and its components are behaving as expected and can prevent defects from entering production. Your automation code itself should be treated with the same development standards as you're putting into product. Quality of automation means trusted delivery. By increasing the quality of the components at deployment time, you can increase the speed at which teams can deliver new value to customers.

Automate manual tasks

This is the "toil" we want to eliminate in the SRE workflow. Examine all places where your engineers are manually manipulating the system. Can this be automated? Start with upgrade and deployment steps. We not only have the opportunity to reduce maintenance windows but also can simultaneously improve the reliability and quality of those updates by automating rote steps, capturing configuration changes as code, and automating quality checks along the way.

Automate resiliency

This is where the power of data and monitoring can feed directly into the automation practice. Evaluate any type of incidents your teams have to respond to with the question, "Could this have been an automated response?" For example, if you've seen a surge in users and needed to spin up new instances to absorb the load, this could be automated. Automation, and feedback loops from data and monitoring, allow you to stay ahead of failures and respond more quickly to changing system conditions. Automated remediation of system failures reduces the cost of failures, avoiding costly incident responses.

START IMPROVING

Adopting SRE practices does not just benefit you with lower-cost system reliability but also increases the agility of your teams to deliver new capabilities and adapt to changes in a complex world. It's important to remember that this is a journey. You won't get there right away. But one key practice, above all others, is essential to making this successful. That is a practice and culture of continuous improvement.

This anchors right back on fundamental Agile and Lean principles. Agile stresses the importance of incremental value and continuous examination and improvement. Lean thinking emphasizes to "seek perfection" in a continuous process of reducing waste and creating flow.

When adopting continuous improvement in SRE, you should focus on two primary measures: the reliability and performance of the system (user experience) and the cost of maintaining the system. There are three continuous improvement practices; we recommend starting off with one and then bringing in the others:

Root cause analysis or incident postmortem
This is performed after an incident response and should be anchored on two key questions: can we prevent this from happening again, or can we reduce the impact of the failure? In general, the answer would lie in either preventing the failure or detecting and mitigating the failure through automation. Here is where your historical data can also be of benefit. Was this a manual error where automation can help? Was there any signal in the data that could have helped us predict this in advance? If so, that's an opportunity. The opportunity may result in a new data measure that can help you predict failure or automate recovery.

Any root cause analysis (RCA) is best done with a constructive blame-free environment. We're here to get it right, not be right, and always seek to improve. Additionally, the RCA should not be treated as a checkbox. A minimum of one action should be taken from any postmortem to try to improve or reduce the impact of any future incident.

Maintenance retrospective
Collect your own data on your maintenance events. How long did it take? Did any problems occur during the maintenance event? In your retrospective, the team can analyze two key questions: how could we have improved the process, and can we automate any steps? Just as with the RCA, we're looking for continuous improvement. Set a goal for the next maintenance event. The goals here are reducing the maintenance time and improving the reliability of the maintenance event. Automation is a friend in this activity as it can help reduce needless manual effort as well as automate recovery or rollback.

Improve performance measures
It is tempting for an engineer to look at their measures and reply to a user report of slow performance. "Well *my* dashboard is green." This is like the proverbial search for keys under the streetlamp. We are seeing only what we've chosen to instrument and monitor. We might be missing something. This can be especially true in the complexity of modern digital systems.

As you start your data and monitoring practice, it is important to recognize you will still need to tune and tweak what you're measuring and how. Your SLIs are only a proxy for the user experience, and over time you will find that there are things you're missing. Here again is where monitoring and historical data come into play. Are the reports of user experiences reflected in your data? Are your SLOs at the right threshold, or perhaps you're missing a key indicator?

In any of your practices, you should ask the following questions:

- Can you make this more efficient or reliable?
- Can you measure and predict failures?
- How can you recover or upgrade the system more quickly?
- How do you improve the digital experience for your users?

This is the practice of continuous improvement. Once you've done so, what more do you need to measure or monitor, what can you automate, and what can you improve? Wash, rinse, repeat.

Cultivating an SRE Culture and Mindset

Mindset and culture are two of the hardest things to define and the most important to get right. In the classic three-legged stool of people, processes, and tools, we still often focus on the tools and processes and expect the people to just follow. But it's not that simple and belies the hard truth. Success is always about how humans work together to deliver results. This requires culture.

Accelerate: Building and Scaling High Performance Technology Organizations (IT Revolution Press) by Nicole Forsgren et al. deeply examines some of the key cultural elements that have been found to be highly correlated to success with SRE. One of these key ingredients is creating a generative culture, one that's anchored in psychological safety and has trust and a learning culture as central elements. When your organization creates an environment of shared responsibility and empowerment, better system reliability outcomes result. Like DevOps, SRE works best when you have a culture that reinforces collaboration and cooperation and stays away from blame and finger-pointing.

On top of a healthy collaborative culture, SRE also demands a particular mindset and understanding of your systems. This might even be characterized as a defensive mindset: what can go wrong will, failures happen, systems will be abused. This is the mindset that introduces topics such as chaos engineering and capacity controls and protects against continuously changing conditions in a complex adaptive system. It is also an ownership mindset that requires the developer to be on call for the service they deploy, and a growth mindset that encourages continuous introspection on how we can do better.

One of the natural questions is, what is the best organizational structure to deliver on this vision? How do we get out of the pattern of developers throwing code over the wall to ops and then ops going through an extended validation process only to throw it back? How do you organize and set expectations to prevent abuse of systems and toxic finger-pointing? There's no one best answer. It is highly dependent on the type of product or services you operate, your engineering maturity, and your risk tolerance. *Team Topologies* by Matthew Skelton and Manuel Pais (IT Revolution Press) has a good discussion of various organizational models and antipatterns around SRE. These are summarized in Table 7-2. In the end, the biggest indicators of success will be the cultural and behavioral norms.

Table 7-2. SRE cultural best practices and antipatterns

Best cultural practice	Antipattern
Everyone feels ownership and has a stake in system reliability.	Throw it over the wall: reliability is "their" problem.
Psychological safety enables challenges to be examined fully.	Finger-pointing and blame culture.
A culture of continuous improvement and a growth mindset.	Status quo and maintenance mindset.

Conclusion

The digital revolution coupled with a global pandemic have put unprecedented pressure on enterprises to modernize and adapt. The rich market for digital services is allowing for unprecedented speed and agility. But the challenges faced in being able to leverage the opportunities these advances have created are daunting, particularly as you look to transform a business built over the years with more traditional IT architectures and organizational models. These challenges range from managing an increasingly complex system with an ever-shifting mesh of connected digital services, to developing a new understanding of reliability. How do you scale your teams as the complexity of this system grows? And how do you start to realize the benefits of speed and agility without getting overrun by chronic stability and management overhead?

Measuring the reliability of a system is no longer a simple formula that calculates uptime. Building a reliable operations practice is not just about having runbooks. Accelerating your development teams means providing higher quality and lowering the risk of more frequent deployments and changes.

The practice of SRE is not the process fad du jour. It is a mindset and a way of working that recognizes and brings tools for the new reality—the complexity of the modern digital enterprise and the need for business resilience and agility. Our traditional models don't scale and cannot meet the needs of today's modern digital architectures. We need a new way of working, and SRE, created and refined by Google, is based on solid time-tested principles of Agile and Lean. We're seeing traction, adoption, and, most important, results.

The fundamental goal as you look to modernize your systems, processes, and organization is to push innovation to the edge and stabilize the core of the system. Complex systems are better managed through data, monitoring, and automation. Setting realistic measures of reliability and the customer experience allows you to invest your energy in the right place. Automation of quality checks and failure remediation allow you to accelerate delivery. Thus, by isolating the core stable services, you can enable and unlock speed at the edge. You unlock innovation and enable accelerated growth.

This is the promise of truly unblocking your development teams and unlocking their capacity while driving efficiency in your operations. Innovation itself requires the ability to take risks. The goal with SRE is not to eliminate risk but to manage it. By reducing the cost of failures, you can unlock the potential of your teams to innovate and accelerate delivery of new business value.

Getting started on your journey can be done by simply starting with a little data, a dab of automation, and a continuous improvement mindset. But just building up an SRE role or organization itself is not enough. You need to look at the organizational culture and structure now to start to understand whether it is conducive to the SRE mindset. Does it allow for all parties to have ownership of reliability, and does it support a growth mindset? In the end, this becomes part of the larger enterprise transformation required to realize the full benefits of a modern digital enterprise.

Afterword: Digital Changes Everything

—Geng Lin, F5 CTO,
and Lori MacVittie, F5 principal technical evangelist

Some of the most popular tourist destinations around the world are cities in which historical buildings still remain. Walk through storied cities across the globe and you will find a mix of old and new architecture that delivers a unique experience for visitors. Even in relatively newer cities you will find aged buildings that have been modernized but retain the rich flavor of their original construction.

This is the task that you have likely undertaken: not to start anew, but to transform an existing architecture into a modern one with the ability to enable a digital business. While the temptation to raze the old and start anew is often strong—after all, technical debt can be as daunting to deal with as financial debt—much is lost in the process.

Archaeologists revel in discovering buried cities of old, driven by the opportunity to better understand the past to guide the future. But as much as archaeologists celebrate such discoveries, they also lament the loss of knowledge that comes from burying the buildings of the past.

This holds true in the enterprise as well. The history of an organization can be read in its current architecture. Throughout the process of modernization, it is important not to lose that history and the insights—and lessons—it provides into business decisions. This is a valuable asset and a more compelling reason to avoid burying it under a new architecture than the obvious cost of starting from scratch.

For example, hidden in the walls of homes built in the 1800s are knob-and-tube electrical wiring systems. This antique technology is inefficient and no longer able to support the modern digital family's drastically higher power needs.

The purpose of the wiring remains the same: to deliver power throughout the home. The material used is simply outdated. Thus updating—modernization—is the correct response, not destruction and rebuilding of the entire home. The same is true for organizations today; it is time to modernize enterprise architecture to support the needs of a digital business:

> Over half of all businesses are under pressure to adapt. The ability to make the right decisions and act swiftly on them will be key to these organizations' post-COVID recovery.[1]

Traditional enterprise architecture frameworks were designed to guide the development of a working—and often unique—enterprise architecture that enables a business to operate efficiently and grow exponentially. A modern enterprise architecture framework must meet that same bar for digital business to maintain its ability to align IT capabilities with a business strategy that increasingly relies on technology.

More important than maintaining alignment is the infusion of adaptability into the business. The goal is not to build something that will last for another 40 years; it is to build something that can adapt for the next century or more. The capabilities established today should support both the technical and business need to adapt to future unknown changes caused by social, economic, and technological shifts. Much like the standing desk, the goal is to establish a *form* that can support the *function* of business—even when the business must change positions over time.

This requirement is the impetus for the inclusion of new domains and disciplines into the enterprise architecture. Without these domains and disciplines, organizations will find it difficult to scale their operations and business at the pace necessary to survive—let alone thrive—in a digital economy.

Technology leaders will need the tools to adapt to the way customers engage in the future, including digital services, omnichannel integration, and extraordinary digital experiences. Given the rapid rate at which many organizations joined the digital economy in response to COVID, it is no surprise that in the first few months of the pandemic, the number of CIOs who believed their company would "fundamentally change the way it engages and interacts with customers" doubled from just 36% to 72%.[2]

---

1 "State of Enterprise Architecture 2021," BIZZdesign, November 2021, *https://oreil.ly/xU7SG*.
2 "Revive the Business in 2021 with Tech-Enabled Transformation," Accenture, *https://oreil.ly/bf1lO*.

An Adaptable Foundation

Primarily, a modernized enterprise architecture will infuse the agility that organizations need to adapt and facilitate that change. Today, just 52% of IT architects believe their organizations can "out-change" the competition.[3] Technology leaders must drive fundamental changes in IT that address the shortcomings that exist in traditional enterprise architecture, especially those that tightly couple digital services and applications to infrastructure and environments and rely on manual processes to make and execute operational decisions.

Of the reasons architects cite as barriers to agility, *leadership* and *legacy IT* are two of the top three. Visionary leadership with a clear picture of how to enable digital business by modernizing architecture can address both barriers and put into place an architecture designed to support a dynamic and distributed digital business. The reality that change is the only constant remains as true as when the Greek philosopher Heraclitus first uttered the words. The "new normal" will be constant change. Unfortunately, most senior business leaders (70%) have no confidence in their organizations' ability to adapt.[4] The version of the enterprise architecture you establish *must* be able to support continuous evolution and adaptation to a constantly changing world and business environment and restore business leaders' confidence.

An enterprise architecture for digital business will have benefits beyond adaptability in a digital economy. An increased use of automation and a shift to embrace SRE practices will enable scale while shifting talent toward innovation and will drive the cost of digital business toward zero. With an average 39% of resources and investments in innovation today, it is difficult to see a future in which organizations have the capacity to adapt at the speed of digital let alone out-change the competition.[5] Embracing practices and approaches that help tip the balance of investments to innovation will produce greater adaptability of IT and the business.

To achieve this, CIOs need to think in terms of capabilities and how they map to and align with business strategy. From there, technology leaders can identify the technologies that will best achieve those capabilities, along with

---

3 BIZZdesign, "State of Enterprise Architecture 2021."
4 Punit Renjen, "Building the Resilient Organization," Deloitte Insights, January 25, 2021, *https://oreil.ly/bksKa*.
5 BIZZdesign, "State of Enterprise Architecture 2021."

organizational changes that enable new ways of working that support those capabilities.

Capabilities to Keep in Mind Moving Forward

To recap the changes needed to accomplish this:

Infrastructure and systems
Necessitated by an accelerated rate of digital transformation driving rapid distribution of society, users, and applications to the cloud and the emerging edge, this domain takes the place of the classical *technical* domain within a traditional enterprise architecture framework. This domain is concerned with delivering systems, network, and storage resources across core, cloud, and edge environments in a unified and more efficient way than its predecessor. It is no longer fixed or static but rather based on dynamic and distributed concepts that allow the elasticity of resources needed to support every other domain.

Security
Security must become its own domain, focusing on infusing secure practices and policies into every other architectural domain. Tools and technologies to enforce policies and provide a digital business with the insights necessary to manage risk vary across domains. Detecting and neutralizing threats remains a broad need, but not at the cost of business. Binary security policies with rigid frameworks will no longer serve the business and, in fact, may impede it. A risk-based approach will provide the necessary balance between security and performance.

Data
Data is an existing domain, with traditional framework elements and policies that work well today. However, the domain must expand to include operational data (telemetry) and new policies and elements that address its unique use to deliver insights that drive automation and decisions across other domains. Traditional policies, too, may require modernization to adjust to emerging regulations and expectations regarding customer/business data privacy.

App delivery
Application delivery is a part of the *technical* domain in a classic enterprise architecture. The practices and technologies associated with app delivery

have evolved and matured since the advent of the internet. They are now necessary to scale, distribute, and deliver the digital assets that represent a modern business: applications. With increasing pressure to improve performance and provide a digital experience that meets users' demanding expectations, the business needs to deliver applications and digital services. This necessitates the elevation of app delivery to its own domain, distinct from the infrastructure it has traditionally been tied to.

Observability and automation

The capability of any living thing to adapt is tied to its ability to receive signals and automatically adjust. Like a living thing, a digital business must have access to as robust a set of digital signals as possible to ensure that it can process, analyze, and subsequently adjust based on internal and external conditions. Observability infuses a digital business with the signals (data) it needs to subsequently adapt with minimal human intervention (automation). The result is a fully functional, closed feedback loop that enables technology leaders to focus on innovation and improvement rather than maintaining core capabilities.

SRE operations

The ability to codify desired business outcomes into SLOs and operate the entirety of a digital service with minimal intervention is a new skill that requires new practices and approaches. These practices and skills are embodied by SRE. Operating a digital business with minimal human intervention implies there remains a need for human governance and, at times, action. SREs fill the need to operate digital businesses based on data by leveraging automation with an eye toward meeting SLOs tied to business outcomes instead of pure technical measures. Adopting SRE operations is a critical, organizational change that is required in order to efficiently operate a digital business and take full advantage of the benefits of data and automation.

We believe an enterprise architecture for digital business, as described throughout this book and illustrated in Figure A-1, will deliver the adaptability needed for the technology to produce tangible business outcomes and drive growth in a digital economy.

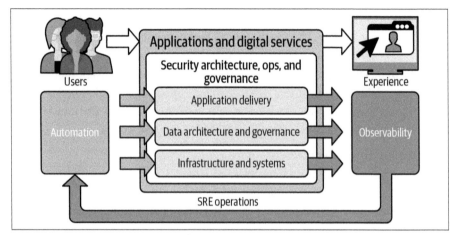

Figure A-1. An enterprise architecture for digital business

The focus of digital transformation has shifted. All eyes are on IT and the technology leaders tasked with enabling their organizations to continue progressing on their digital transformation journey. The CIO is now in the digital transformation driver's seat. Modernizing IT by establishing a new standard—an enterprise architecture for digital business—will be the best way to successfully navigate the route to becoming a digital business.

About the Contributors

This book would not be possible without the expertise and dedication of its contributing authors.

JOEL MOSES, F5 CTO OF SYSTEMS AND DISTINGUISHED ENGINEER

Joel Moses is currently serving as the CTO of Systems at F5, as well as attaining the rank of distinguished engineer. He has over 30 years of industry experience in the cybersecurity and networking fields.

Prior to joining F5, he designed large-scale security and infrastructure architectures for consulting clients and served as the lead US security and infrastructure architect for one of the largest accounting/consulting firms in the world. At F5, he is a founding member of the Office of the CTO and is principally responsible for advanced research, intellectual property, proofs of concept, and strategic studies related to security, hardware, and cloud technologies. He holds several US patents related to encryption techniques.

MIKE CORRIGAN, F5 VP OF ENGINEERING

Mike Corrigan is the VP of Engineering for Technology Excellence in the Office of the CTO. He has established the corporate Technology Excellence Initiative to enable the developer organization to grow through talent excellence, innovation excellence, and technical influence. Prior to this, he led the initial SaaS transformation of F5 and was responsible for building the initial corporate SaaS platform and some of the initial key SaaS offerings. In addition, Mike had engineering responsibility for the initial analytics and AI platforms. Prior to joining the Office of the CTO, he led the development of the F5 management product BIG-IQ for the BIG-IP platform.

Mike brings deep subject-matter expertise in cloud services, SaaS, and analytics with 20+ years of experience following the trajectory of the ever-evolving internet/cloud/analytics technology spaces. Before joining F5 in 2015, he held GM and engineering leadership roles at Microsoft, Cisco, MITRE, and INRIX. In addition, he has a strong history of leadership in start-ups in the ecommerce, analytics, and cloud spaces.

Mike holds a BS in electrical and computer engineering from Clarkson University. He is an avid adventure traveler, wildlife photographer, marathoner, and diver.

JAMES HENDERGART, F5 DIRECTOR OF DEVELOPMENT OPERATIONS

James Hendergart is the director of Development Operations in the Office of the CTO. In his role, he sets the operational cadence of the Office of the CTO, including budgeting, executive hiring, All-Hands presentations, and the Project Management Office. James has been at F5 for over 10 years and has served in many roles in the Business Development organization and in the Office of the CTO.

Prior to F5, James was at Microsoft for almost 10 years and served in many roles, including account management, program and product management, and technology specialist. He holds a BA in international studies from Pepperdine University.

He lives in Bend, Oregon, with his wife and three daughters and enjoys exploring the outdoors and frequent visits to the Oregon coast.

KEN ARORA, DISTINGUISHED ENGINEER, F5 OFFICE OF THE CTO

Ken Arora is a distinguished engineer in F5's Office of the CTO, focusing on how the evolving principles and mindset required to address emerging cybersecurity threats can be reduced to practice across a variety of relevant application security subdomains—from identity to API to workload compromise. Ken advances technologies at F5 including intelligent data ingestion and analytics in the pursuit of identification and mitigation of advanced threats, targeted use of hardware acceleration to achieve higher efficacy at lower cost, and the design of intent-driven, workflow-centric user experiences. Ken is also a thought leader in the evolution of the zero trust mindset for security as modern applications evolve to use more third-party code and services and to be increasingly distributed.

Prior to F5, Ken cofounded a company that developed a solution for ASIC-accelerated pattern matching, which was then acquired by Cisco, where he was the technical architect for the Cisco ASA product family. In his more distant past, he was also the architect for several Intel microprocessors. His undergraduate degrees are in astrophysics and electrical engineering, from Rice University.

Ken enjoys playing hockey, but when off the ice, he also spends time on the board of Silicon Valley Shakespeare and is a superforecaster for the Good Judgment Project.

MICHAEL WILEY, F5 VP OF ENGINEERING AND CTO OF APPLICATIONS

Michael Wiley joined F5 in early 2020 as VP of Engineering and CTO of Applications. Previously, he served as executive director of JP Morgan Chase, where he led firm-wide application frameworks, platform observability, toolchain, and business analytics teams.

Prior to JP Morgan and F5, Michael was the software engineering leader for Google's Next Billion Users (BU). There he led multiple cloud products and solutions, serving emerging markets aligned to Google's initiative to optimize application performance and accelerate internet adoption. Michael's leadership in production, corporate networks, operations, acquisitions, software, and SRE teams brought significant changes to the way Google operates today.

Michael has been leading engineering teams in markets across the world for many years. His vast knowledge of consumer, enterprise, and service provider scaling demands and challenges have been central to his career, from Cisco to starting his own business, to Google, and now within the F5 family.

With a decade-long career in the US Navy as a flight engineer, 20 years in technology leadership, living on three continents, traveling to 24 countries, and being a father of six, Michael brings a unique customer-centric perspective, action-oriented problem solving, scaling teams, and organizational structure that will ensure F5 leadership in the marketplace.

JULIA RENOUARD, F5 VP OF ENGINEERING

Julia is a VP of Engineering at F5, where she has led teams for the past 10 years. She cut her engineering teeth on networking and security, including helping launch a start-up building a VPN that delivers mobile users' optimized experience. Her tenure and contributions at F5 have spanned from service provider technology to cloud native, participating in the integration of NGINX into F5.

As a leader in the Office of the CTO at F5, she leads a Common Engineering team to secure, enable, and accelerate execution for all teams with a full set of engineering services and enablers.

In her spare time, she is dedicated to advancing the participation of women in engineering careers, supporting local schools, and working to improve access to the outdoors. She studied computer science at the University of Washington and is a dedicated Pacific Northwesterner who has raised two daughters and enjoys hiking, backpacking, and camping.

Index

Symbols

5 × 9s concept, 113

A

access control
    as policy building blocks, 80-83
    definition of term, 67
    in terms of user identity, 70
Acorn RISC Machine, 28
adaptability, 45-47, 131
adaptive security strategy, 76
Agile practices, 42
agility, 129
AI-assisted attack tools, 75
AI-assisted business, ix
AI-assisted diagnostic tools, 84
AISecOps, 84-85
anomaly detection, 84
application delivery
    app delivery in modernized architecture, 47
    as new domain of digital enterprise architecture, 14, 130
    challenges of emerging technologies, 38
    impact on adaptability, 45-47

impact on infrastructure, 20
lack of in traditional enterprise architecture, 38
modern applications, 40-42
role of app delivery in digital services, 42-45
traditional applications, 39
application domain
    impact of digital transformation on, 10
    in digital enterprise architecture, 13
    in traditional architectures, 5
application security (see security)
application traces, 93
architecture framework, 4
ARM processors, 28-31
asset governance maturity, 79
authentication
    as policy building block, 80-83
    definition of term, 67
    in modern applications, 70
    multifactor, 73
auto-instrumentation, 97
automatable app delivery, 48
automation and observability
    AI-enhanced decision making, 101
    as new domain of digital enterprise architecture, 15, 131

automation in digital businesses, 102
evaluation steps for automating activities, 105
need for instrumentation, 94-99
relationship between, 103-105
SRE operations and, 119, 121
telemetry collection and management, 99-101
telemetry data types, 91-94
value of to digital businesses, 88-90
availability, 72, 115

B

Booch, Grady, 1
business availability, 72, 115
business domain
impact of digital transformation on, 9
in digital enterprise architecture, 13
in traditional architecture, 5
business goals, 88-90

C

castle-and-moat approach, 73
CDN (content delivery network) providers, 7
change failure rates, 111
CISC (complex instruction set computer), 32
Cloud Native Computing Foundation (CNCF), 25
code releases, quality of, 89
complex instruction set computer (CISC), 32
compute layer blind spots, 54
conformance checking, 70
content delivery network (CDN) providers, 7

Content Security Policies, 23
continuous improvement, 119
Conway's law
application delivery and, 43
definition of term, 37
modern applications and, 41
traditional applications and, 39
cost awareness and impact, 89
COVID-19 pandemic
acceleration of digital transformation due to, vi, viii, 6-8, 125
fundamental changes brought on by, 128
shift to SRE practices due to, 110
crawl, walk, run application journey, 68
credential fraud, 73
credential stuffing attacks, 75
customer experience, 89

D

data analysis, 58
data architecture and governance
as new domain of digital enterprise architecture, 15, 130
data pipelines and practices, 57-61
drawbacks of traditional architectures, 52
evolution of data governance, 62-64
operational data platforms, 52-57
potential of operational data, 51
privacy and sovereignty, 61
data domain
application delivery and, 13
impact of digital transformation on, 10
in traditional architectures, 6
data processing units (DPUs), 33
data science, 58

data scientists, 58
data silos, 95
Davis, Martin, 22
DDoS mitigation, 71, 71
defense-in-depth approach, 73
denial-of-service (DOS) attack, 71
deployment frequency, 111
deterministic enforcement tools, 67, 70
DevOps Research and Assessment
    (DORA), 111
differential privacy, 62
digital enterprise architecture
    framework for, 13
    new domains of, 14, 130
    traditional domains of, 12
    trends indicating need for, 6-9
digital expansion, ix
digital identities, 9
digital services
    accelerating delivery of value through,
        111
    adaptability and, 129
    balancing cost versus performance, 19
    boosting resilience of, 97
    challenges of, 125
    changes needed to support, 131
    definition of term, 87
    failures during COVID-19 pandemic, 7
    functions critical to, 38, 42-45, 49
    in digital enterprise architecture frame-
        work, 12-16
    response time of, 101
    scaling, 44, 47
    scaling and securing, 10
    significant data generated by, 11
    support required by, 9

understanding infrastructure health
    and status, 19, 26, 36, 88, 94
user experience and, 107, 128
digital transformation
    capacity to engage in innovation, v
    challenges of, 11
    critical technologies/capabilities, x, 130
    F5's ability to provide insight into, xii
    forces behind, v
    impact on architecture, 9-11
    infrastructure prior to, 19
    key issues inhibiting, vii
    respecting history of organizations, 127
    role of adaptability in, 128-130
    role of technology in, viii
    trends indicating need for, 6-9
digital workforce, 6
distributed tracing, 93
domain-specific compute, 32
DORA (DevOps Research and Assess-
    ment), 111
DOS (denial-of-service) attack, 71
DPUs (data processing units), 33

E

edge computing
    digital expansion and, x
    emergence of technologies and tooling
        for, 18
    increase in enterprise-generated data
        created by, 8
    real-time decision making and, 59
    standards for, 26
enterprise architecture (see also digital
    enterprise architecture)
    challenges of modernizing, 11
    emergence of architectural standards, 4

four domains of traditional, 5
framework for, 4
impact of digital transformation on,
9-11
role of standardization in innovation,
2-4
transforming from physical to digital, 1
trends creating need for new digital
framework, 6-9, 87
enterprise data practice, 52, 64
(see also data architecture and governance)
errors, 121

F
file access, 73
Floyer, David, 31
form follows function, 1, 10, 87, 128
four golden signals, 121

G
global pandemic (see COVID-19 pandemic)
graphics processing units (GPUs), 32

I
identity fraud, 9, 73, 75
IETF (Internet Engineering Task Force),
24
incident postmortems, 123
incremental operational models, 42
indirect attacks, 74
infrastructure and systems
as new domain of digital enterprise
architecture, 15, 130
changes to traditional IT approach, 18
emerging problem sets, 31-33

enabling new technologies and standards, 27-31
evolutions driving change in, 20
impact of standardization on, 22-27
impact of third wave of the internet on,
17
importance of performance, 19
prior to digital transformation, 19
xPU digital enterprise architecture,
33-35
innovation
capacity to engage in, v
role of standardization in, 2-4
innovation equation, v
instruction set architecture (ISA), 28
instrumentation
need for in observability, 94
obstacles to, 96
surmounting challenges to, 97-99
intellectual property, 79
interactive architectures, 40
Internet Engineering Task Force (IETF),
24
ISA (instruction set architecture), 28

L
latency, 121
latency rates, 73
lateral-motion attacks, 74
lead time, 111
legacy IT, 129
logging, 93
low-and-slow preexploitation phase, 75

M
machine learning algorithms, 74
maintenance retrospective, 123

message delivery, 43

metrics, 92

MFA (multifactor authentication), 73

microservices, 21, 41, 96

missing data, 95

mobile computing

    impact on app delivery, 46

    impact on cloud computing, 40

    impact on infrastructure, 21

    lack of representation of in traditional architectures, 44

monitoring, 120

monitoring capabilities, 25

Moore's law, 31

multicloud environments, 45

multifactor authentication (MFA), 73

N

network interface card (NIC), 33

nonproxy vantage points, 54

O

observable app delivery, 49 (see also automation and observability)

Open Group Architecture Framework, The (TOGAF), 4, 6

open source projects, 74

Open Systems Interconnection (OSI), 44

OpenTelemetry (OTEL), 25, 94, 98, 119

operational data (see also data architecture and governance)

    inventorying application components, 53-56

    potential of, 51

    qualities necessary for enterprise data practice, 52, 56

    understanding new data sources, 53

operational objectives, 88-90

operations domain, 13

optimization, 90

OSI (Open Systems Interconnection), 44

OTEL (OpenTelemetry), 25, 94, 98, 119

P

pandemic (see COVID-19 pandemic)

performance measurements, 94, 123

personally identifiable information (PII), 24

portable app delivery, 49

postmortems, 123

privacy

    differential privacy, 62

    digital transformation and, 23

    granularity of access control, 62

    role in data governance, 61

Q

Quick UDP Internet Connection (QUIC), 24

R

ransomware, 72

rate limiting, 73

RCA (root cause analysis), 123

reduced instruction set computer (RISC), 28

refactoring, 96

reliability

    versus availability, 113

    impact of subtle changes on, 114

    new understanding of, 117

    SRE practices and, 111, 125

    uptime as a measurement of, 90

request rates, 73

RISC (reduced instruction set computer), 28

risk management, 90

risk, shared by consumers, 9

risk-aware remediation policies, 67, 73-78

root cause analysis (RCA), 123

rule-based systems, 74

S

Samsung, 29

saturation, 121

scaling

    challenges of, 7

    digital services, 10, 44, 47

    requirements for digital business, 87

scope, 62

security

    applying protection to assets, 66

    as new domain of digital enterprise architecture, 15, 130

    crawl, walk, run application journey, 68

    from concept to practice, 78-85

    generalized deterministic enforcement, 70

    impact of standardization on, 23-25

    inventorying key digital assets, 66

    prioritizing, 86

    proactive approach to, 86

    proportional protections and, 86

    risk-aware remediations, 73-78

    risk-reward perspective, 65, 86

    situational awareness, 71-73

    technologies used, 67

    understanding exposure and access, 66

    zero-trust approach, 83

security domain, 13

security policy, 80

service-level agreements (SLAs), 114

service-level indicators (SLIs), 115

service-level objectives (SLOs), 114

Session Initiation Protocol (SIP), 23

Simple Network Management Protocol (SNMP), 71

SIP (Session Initiation Protocol), 23

site reliability engineering (SRE) (see SRE operations)

situational awareness tools, 67, 71-73

SLAs (service-level agreements), 114

SLIs (service-level indicators), 115

SLOs (service-level objectives), 114

Slowloris, 71

smart healthcare devices, 100

smart homes/smart devices, 8

smart NICs, 33

SNMP (Simple Network Management Protocol), 71

span IDs, 93

specialized computing

    domain-specific compute, 32

    transparent assistive compute, 33

specialized processing units, 32

SRE operations

    as new domain of digital enterprise architecture, 16, 131

    balancing speed with quality, 116

    best practices and antipatterns, 125

    core principles of, 117-119

    cultivating SRE culture and mindset, 124

    effectiveness of, 111-113

    getting started in, 119-124, 126

    goals of, 117, 126

    managing complexity and increasing speed through, 110-111

need for in digital businesses, 107-110
practices and tools of, 119
reliability versus availability, 113-116
standardization
emergence of architectural standards, 4
impact on infrastructure and systems, 22-27
notable moments in, 2
role in innovation, 2
system calls, 73

T

Taiwan Semiconductor Manufacturing Company (TSMC), 29
task automation, ix
technical domain
application delivery and, 13
changes to traditional IT approach, 18
impact of digital transformation on, 10
in traditional architectures, 6
telemetry data
collection and management of, 99-101
need for instrumentation, 94-99
standardizing format of, 25
types of, 91-94
The Open Group Architecture Framework (TOGAF), 4, 6
third-party components, 55
threat surfaces, inside applications, 73
time to market, 89
time to restore service, 111
timestamps, 93
TOGAF (The Open Group Architecture Framework), 4, 6
traceroutes, 94

traces, 93
traffic, 121
transactional architectures, 39
transparent assistive compute, 33
TSMC (Taiwan Semiconductor Manufacturing Company), 29

U

user activity monitoring, 24

V

Vellante, Dave, 31
velocity, 89
vendor-neutral application libraries, 97
visibility
enhancing, 77
lack of, 25
Voice over IP, 23

W

WAAP (web app and API protection), 46
Wasm (WebAssembly), 27
Web 2.0, 41
web app and API protection (WAAP), 46
WebAssembly (Wasm), 27
World Wide Web Consortium (W3C), 23

X

xPU class of infrastructure, 33-35

Z

Zachman Framework, 4
zero-trust approach, 83

About the Authors

Geng Lin is executive vice president and chief technology officer at F5. He is responsible for leading technology strategy, product evolution, and critical innovations for the company.

Lin is an industry-leading expert in distributed systems, software defined infrastructure, and cloud services. He is a contributing author of two books on cloud and data-intensive computing. He has published many technical papers and holds nine US patents.

Lori MacVittie is a technologist and principal technical evangelist in F5's Office of the CTO with an emphasis on emerging architectures and technologies including cloud and edge computing, digital transformation, automation and orchestration, microservices, and application delivery. MacVittie has over 25 years of industry experience spanning application development, IT architecture, and network and systems operation.

Prior to joining F5, MacVittie was an award-winning technology editor at *Network Computing Magazine*. As an enterprise architect, she drove architectural efforts to lead a global transportation and logistics firm into the Internet age, and has developed software for Nokia phones, Autodesk, and regional telecommunications firms. She coauthored the CADD profile for ANSI NCITS 320-1998 and holds a US patent for application delivery provisioning. MacVittie is a contributing author of books on cloud security and object-oriented development and has authored books on application security and XAML.

Colophon

The cover design is by Susan Thompson. The cover fonts are Guardian Sans and Gilroy Semibold. The text fonts are Scala Pro, Benton Sans, and Minion Pro; the heading font is Benton Sans; and the code font is Ubuntu Mono.

Lightning Source UK Ltd.
Milton Keynes UK
UKHW022244170822
407450UK00005B/13